Leaders of Faith

Empowering Muslim Youth with Skills
to Inspire, Lead and Achieve

SARAH GULFRAZ

Copyright © 2025 Sarah Gulfraz

Sarah Gulfraz has asserted her right to be identified as the author of this Work in accordance with the Copyright, Designs and Patents Act 1988.

All rights reserved.

No portion of this book may be reproduced in any form, stored in a retrieval system, stored in a database, or published/transmitted in any form or by any means, electronic, mechanical, photocopying, recording or otherwise, without prior written permission of the publisher.

Dedication

~ **Bismillah** ~

May Allah (swt) accept our efforts and grant us success in this life and the next. Ameen.

In dedication to my loving family and all their support.

Contents

1. Introduction — 1
2. Introduction to Muslim Youth Leadership — 4
3. Characteristics of a Muslim Youth Leader — 13
4. Inspirational Examples of Youth Leadership in Islamic History — 26
5. Youth Leadership in the Quran and Sunnah — 37
6. Building Confidence and Resilience in Youth Leaders — 49
7. Youth Engagement in Community Service and Activism — 58
8. Leadership Skills Development for Muslim Youth — 64
9. Ethical Leadership and Islamic Values — 75
10. Mentorship and Role Modelling for Youth Leaders — 87
11. Empowering Muslim Youth for a Promising Future — 99
12. Conclusion — 105

Find Out More — 107

Chapter One

Introduction

In this modern world, leadership is more than just a title or position. It's about realising who we are at our core and applying that understanding to all we do. This is the inner leader's path. It's a path that is both important and always misinterpreted. The idea of an inner leader journey is frequently ignored in a society that is obsessed with action and quick outcomes. Many people don't understand this path. About getting things done, it appears too intangible and possibly meaningless.

In an ever-evolving world, Muslims are at a unique crossroads. They have to deal with the global landscape filled with growth opportunities, digital tools, innovation, and connectivity. At the same time, they grapple with unique struggles like cultural clashes and racism and handle the constant battle to balance faith with modern expectations. Sometimes in life, even outside of work, you might need to use your leadership abilities to encourage people around you.

There are undoubtedly certain persons who possess qualities that make them excellent leaders from birth. Those with an extroverted disposition can take the initiative and feel more at ease around other people. However, it's crucial to remember that many leadership abilities can be acquired over time. To succeed, all you need is the proper instruction and commitment.

Muslim leaders are born with powerful beliefs, and they can be change makers with the help of the right tools, guidance, and inspiration.

Moreover, they can rise above limitations, lead with conviction, and shape a better world rooted in compassion, justice, and truth.

The book is both a call to action and an invitation to self-discovery for every young person who has ever wondered, "Is it possible for me to make a difference?" – because the answer is a resounding yes. For Muslims, a strong faith in Allah (SWT) and the guidance drawn from the life of the Holy Prophet (PBUH) provide a foundation stronger than any storm.

Leadership is a vital ability that not only empowers people but also fortifies communities and society overall. There has never been a greater need for effective leadership in today's quickly changing world. Especially for our young people, they have the capacity to significantly influence the world around us and serve as our future leaders.

Youth have always been at the forefront of positive change in Islamic history. Many of the companions of Prophet Muhammad (PBUH) were young individuals in the early days of Islam. This was largely due to his regard for the young people in his neighbourhood. He never ignored or made them feel inferior, regardless of how busy he was. When younger people approached him for advice, the Holy Prophet (PBUH) took the time to greet them with grace. Many youthful companions of the Holy Prophet (PBUH) were not just followers but also exemplary leaders. Like their elders, they served as role models for their community and still serve as an inspiration to young Muslims today.

The Muslim youth of today ought to be motivated to appreciate this rich heritage. The young people have consistently felt that their opinions are unappreciated and their voices are unheard. They frequently wish to contribute to social change and the country's advancement, but they are frequently denied the means and chance to do so. Islam empowers them from the start. The Quran and Sunnah highlight numerous young individuals who stood firm in their faith, challenged falsehood, and took responsibility far beyond their years. Their lives prove that age is no barrier when one's heart is anchored in purpose and truth.

Our lives are deeply ingrained with digital technology. We appreciate its extreme convenience and sense its enormous advantages. Because technology is developing so quickly, we are the first generation of parents who must figure out how to properly supervise our kids' use of digital devices.

But in the Muslim community, we also need to take into account the possibility that excessive technology use could harm the spiritual growth of the kids we want to raise into self-assured, fruitful Muslims. Participating in your child's digital life as a Muslim parent can help you better understand what they are exposed to and offer assistance when necessary.

Growing up in a world shaped by constant digital exposure, cultural shifts, and global challenges presents both trials and opportunities. Muslim youth often find themselves torn between the values of their faith and the pressures of society. They may struggle to reconcile tradition with trends or to find a voice that speaks authentically in a world that demands conformity.

This book aims to prepare Muslim youth to maintain a balance between tradition and modernity. It provides detailed guidance for Muslim youth to lead without deviating from pure faith in Islam. As you turn the pages of this book, you realise that you're living your dream. So let your imagination be purely guided by the light of faith and the possibilities that lie ahead. Reflect deeply, act boldly, and grow continually. Each chapter will challenge, inspire, and prepare you to become the leader you are born to be.

Remember, the best leaders are not those who seek power, but those who seek to empower others. Let this be your legacy—not of fame or fortune, but of faith, service, and lasting impact. You are the future, and the future needs you. So rise. Step forward with confidence. Lead with heart. And let the world see what it truly means to be a Leader of Faith.

Chapter Two

Introduction to Muslim Youth Leadership

Importance of Youth Leadership in Islam

In any community, youth are considered an essential component. They can create amazing changes that will make society kinder and more empathetic since they are the next generation. Islam emphasises the value of raising our children rightly because the most important period of a human's life is when we are young. It's the period when the direction we get moulds our perspective on the world and personal development.

When children are nurtured with care and made aware of the Islamic teachings, they grow into youth who serve as useful assets to their families and the wider community. More than anyone else, our beloved Prophet Muhammad (PBUH) recognised the significance of believing in and caring for the youngest members of his community.

"Take benefit of five before five: your youth before your old age, your health before your sickness, your wealth before your poverty, your free time before you are busy, and your life before your death" (Sahih Al-Albani)

Being young is a stage of life that encourages productivity and creativity. Young people are important resources for a country's growth since their minds are usually more active and receptive to innovative ideas. The role of youth is especially important in the modern world, when global security and technical breakthroughs are at the forefront.

This stage is full of energy and the potential to aim and achieve anything. Islam encourages utilising that phase for leadership and legacy-building. Being a leader is a trait that cuts across age, race, and religion. It's an essential ability that benefits communities and society overall and empowers individuals. There has never been a greater need for effective leadership in today's quickly changing world.

Integrating Islamic ideas into leadership development can unlock the potential of Muslim youth. The Quran and Prophet Muhammad's (PBUH) teachings provide insightful advice on leadership and the place of youth in society.

Quranic Verses and Hadiths Emphasising the Role of Youth in Society

Since then, young people have been essential to the globalisation and proliferation of Islam. Therefore, it's impossible to overstate the importance of youth in Islam. Numerous times throughout the Quran, especially in the narratives of prophets and other notable people, the value of youth is underlined.

Youth play a vital and crucial role in all domains, whether political, economic, social, national, scientific, or information-related. History has shown that even in the past, young people have been at the forefront of both minor and major changes. It is impossible to overestimate the influence of young people on the future. Their enthusiasm, ingenuity, and inventiveness are crucial for advancing development and producing favourable results for society as a whole.

According to the Holy Quran, human existence is divided into three basic phases: childhood, when one is weak and dependent; youth, when one is strong and capable; and old age, when one becomes weak again. According to this framework, the Quran uses a variety of terms and idioms to allude to the youth phase, some of which are listed below:

> *"He is the One who created you from dust, then from a sperm-drop, then from a clinging clot; then He brings you forth as an infant, so that you may reach your full strength, and eventually become elderly." (Quran 40:67)*

When someone reaches both physical and mental maturity, a state usually associated with youth, they are said to be "reaching full strength." This verse asserts that youth is the apex of previous stages and a normal period in the human lifecycle.

Islam aims to train young people in three important areas: ethics, beliefs, and religious practices. It also lays out specific obligations for them in each of these areas, acknowledging young people's enormous potential and talents. Doing this gives individuals a structure for their spiritual and material lives that aligns with the intent of creation and guides them towards enduring happiness.

Moreover, the Quran clearly describes the role of youth through the example of the companions of the Prophet Muhammad (PBUH):

> *"We narrate their original story to you." (Quran 12:3)*

It speaks of a group of young people who had faith in their Lord. By claiming to believe in the Lord of the Worlds, these young people risked looking directly into the eyes of the oppressive rulers of their day. Their story, as told by Allah (SWT), reflects their bravery, unshakeable faith, and universal declaration.

> *"We made their hearts strong when they stood up and declared that our Lord is He Who is the Lord of the heavens and the earth, and we worship no other God besides Him. Will not call. If we do that, we will be talking in vain." (Quran 18:14)*

Similarly, certain young people who believed in Hazrat Musa (AS) were named in the Holy Quran. Only a small number of young individuals in dire situations professed their confidence in the prophetic role of Hazrat Musa (AS), despite the fact that the populace rejected him in every manner.

> *"None believed Moses except a few youths from this nation, because of the fear of Pharaoh and the fear of the leaders of their own people that Pharaoh would punish them." (Quran 10:83)*

Islam demands that young people maintain their *taqwa* (piety and God-consciousness) and be mindful of God while they are at the height of their physical and spiritual abilities.

> *"God is proud of a young person who does not fall into temptation." (Bihar al-Anwar)*

No matter what country, youth are regarded as the foundation. The morality of its youth determines the degree of civilisation, moral development, and the consolidation of power and authority. One may argue that nations endure as long as their morals endure. The overwhelming numerical weight of young people and their relatively recent entry into the public sphere, along with a global wave of Islamic revivalism, are the current causes of the youth and Islam debate. Youth are essential to any society's future and play a crucial role in growth and decline. The rationale is that young people's roles as individuals and engaged members of society have the power to either brighten or darken the future.

Islam views youth as a period of vitality, moral development, and accountability. Young people were empowered by the Prophet Muhammad (PBUH), who equipped them to teach and lead.

> *"Go to your people, stay with them, teach them, and give them (my) orders." (Al-Bukhari)*

The youth are this Ummah's future; they are the ambassadors of Islam, spreading its message to the following generation. The purpose of the young is to spread the divine word of Islam throughout the world. Youth represents the future; it signifies that the Ummah can reclaim its position as a leader and may take pride in its future. The Ummah's future leaders will be today's Muslim youngsters. Their families, educational institutions, and society should all prepare them for this position.

Significance of Nurturing Leadership Skills among Young Muslims

The ability to lead, inspire and motivate people towards a common objective or vision is known as leadership. Good leaders set goals, mould conduct, and encourage dedication. A variety of compelling factors highlight the significance of leadership, which spans personal, organisational, and social levels.

Successful leaders create an atmosphere of passion and steadfast dedication by inspiring and motivating others. They foster an environment that inspires people to reach their greatest potential and pursue greatness. Leaders steer people, groups, and organisations towards shared objectives by offering compelling vision and unambiguous guidance. They guarantee alignment, provide direction, and establish purpose.

By giving constructive criticism and promoting both professional and personal growth, leaders assist and guide individuals and groups. Being a leader is accepting responsibility for one's actions and results. Leaders take accountability for their choices and act with honesty and morality. Success and development are facilitated by leadership. Goals are achieved, performance is improved, and favourable results are obtained through good leadership.

In sum, developing young Muslims' leadership abilities is crucial to producing people who can benefit their local communities and society at large. Investing in leadership development not only gives them the ability to handle the challenges of the contemporary world, but it also guarantees a future marked by accountability, fortitude, and significant contributions to humanity and faith.

Islamic leadership includes the duty and confidence placed on people to lead and assist others in accordance with Islamic values. Leaders must be knowledgeable, wise, and competent while upholding accountability, justice, and integrity. The importance of leadership transcends communities, governments, enterprises, and individual growth. Effectiveness, engagement, and general well-being are all greatly impacted. By adopting competent leadership, people and civilisations can overcome obstacles, advance, and build a brighter future.

Islamic leadership serves the common good and fosters well-being by fusing moral principles, spiritual direction, and pragmatic abilities. It acknowledges the harmony between material obligations and spiritual development. Leaders inspire and have a beneficial impact on others by adhering to Islamic values and exhibiting virtues, which promote community and unity. Islamic leadership is based on core principles ingrained in Islamic doctrine. These principles shape leaders' interactions and contributions to the community. In the later section of this book, we will discuss some important traits that Muslim youth should cultivate to be successful in their professional and personal lives.

Challenges and Opportunities for Muslim Youth Leaders

Muslim youth leaders are situated at the nexus of faith and practicality, tradition and modernity, local expectations and international impact. They play a rigorous and dynamic role. Muslims have contributed to astronomy, medicine, philosophy, architecture, and many other disciplines.

However, the growth of Islamophobia has put Muslim youth on the defensive by portraying Islam as aggressive, illogical, and incompatible with modern society. They face unique obstacles that put their fortitude and vision to the test as they negotiate leadership roles both inside and outside of their communities. They are also uniquely positioned to create inclusive futures based on moral principles, bridge generational gaps, and effect positive change.

Identifying Unique Challenges Faced by Muslim Youth in Leadership Roles

The biggest obstacle facing Muslim adolescents, mostly in Western societies today, is the difficulty of defining their Islamic identity. These young people are facing a fight that jeopardises their social and psychological stability due to mounting cultural, political, and economic pressures. They have to balance their religious beliefs with the expectations of society, which causes a rift where some people lose their religion while others become radical.

Identity is all about belonging to a religion, a language, a set of morals, a country, a gender, a group, or other associations. This sense of belonging must be solidly created and established. If this basis is flawed, identity uncertainty or an identity crisis results.

It is not necessary to isolate or detach from other cultures and religions to maintain one's religious identity. Rather, a Muslim ought to set a good example, dispelling the falsehoods that have been unjustly attached to Islam and Muslims. The monotheistic philosophy, which forms the basis of a Muslim's essential beliefs and dictates their relationships with others as well as their appearance, is the source of Islamic identity.

The identity crisis among Muslim youth is being exacerbated by three primary factors. Because of prejudice and persecution, many Muslim adolescents are constantly afraid to expose their Islamic identity, which keeps them from fully engaging in their religious rites.

They lack the understanding that would bolster their faith and confidence in the life of the Prophet Muhammad (PBUH) and his companions; they don't fully understand the magnificence of our religion, and they do not know Allah (SWT). They are therefore ineligible to adhere to this religion and fulfil its responsibilities because they have no affiliation with it.

Furthermore, the majority of Muslim youth in the West experience intergenerational conflict, feeling torn between the Western society, which rejects them and views them as outsiders, which exacerbates their sense of alienation and lack of belonging, and the generation of immigrant parents who do not fully comprehend their issues and force them to adhere to a religion that appears incompatible with their way of life and the societies around them.

Young people must be taught the genuine Islamic faith away from the false stereotypes that misrepresent it. To take pride in and defend their Islamic identity, they must learn the proper creed, the honourable history of the Prophet (PBUH), and the tales of the great companions and followers.

Another significant obstacle is visibility and representation. Muslim teenagers may find it difficult to identify role models who share their views and experiences in various leadership fields, particularly in the public, political, or corporate sectors. As a result of this lack of visibility, it may be more difficult for them to overcome glass ceilings or feel secure in their capacity to lead successfully.

Navigating the demands of their families, communities, and societies is one of the most difficult tasks facing Muslim adolescents. Anxiety and stress are frequently brought on by the need to perform well academically, uphold religious beliefs, and conform to cultural norms. Expectations from the community can be a source of inspiration and a hindrance. Muslim youngsters may experience pressure to "prove" that they are well-integrated, modern people, which could weaken their Islamic identity.

For Muslim adolescents, mental health is yet another important concern. Their mental health may suffer significantly as a result of identity issues, social isolation, and Islamophobia. Accessing mental health treatments can be difficult for Muslim kids as well, especially if they believe that the services are insensitive to their culture or do not recognise their unique needs. Anxiety, depression, loneliness, and, in certain situations, an unwillingness to ask for help might result from this lack of support.

Lastly, there may be restrictions on access to platforms and resources. Systemic obstacles prevent many Muslim adolescents from receiving high-quality education, mentorship, or money for projects they want to spearhead. This problem worsens in areas with political unrest, poverty, or discrimination. Every obstacle presents an opportunity for development. Armed with courage, imagination, and conviction, Muslim student leaders have the power to change perceptions, build stronger communities, and open the door to a more morally upright and inclusive world.

Chapter Three

Characteristics of a Muslim Youth Leader

Quranic Principles and Values Shaping Effective Leadership

In Islam, leadership is essentially a trust (Amanah). It symbolises a psychological agreement between a leader and his followers that he will do everything he can to protect, guide, and treat them justly. As a result, doing the right thing is the main focus of Islamic leadership. In Islam, effective leadership is firmly rooted in the Quran's teachings.

According to the Quran, understanding Islamic leadership or the Islamic leadership paradigm requires knowledge that predates the creation of humanity. Both the internal and external aspects of Islamic leadership become apparent when one understands the meaning of these passages. It teaches that education, humility, and faith in God are the foundations of effective leadership. Beyond power, it demands moral accountability and spiritual consciousness as a khalifah on earth.

These verses' core themes will help someone understand the esoteric aspects of Islamic leadership and its exoteric aspects. While esoteric refers to the inner aspects of Islamic leadership, such as the ideals, its relationship to the Sacred, and Allah's (SWT) sovereignty, exoteric refers to the external aspects of leadership, such as conduct, procedure, and talent.

Traditional definitions of leadership, which describe it as a process, ability, skill, or behaviour, exhibit exoteric characteristics. The philosophy, concept, and fundamental principles of Islam are the esoterical aspects of Islamic leadership, but the observable and rational elements that result from them are the esoterical examples. For example, a Muslim leader uses the concepts and values derived from Islam's philosophy, concept, and fundamental values to guide his people through empowerment (Tafwid) and deliberation (Shura).

In the Holy Quran, Allah (SWT) refers to people as his emissaries or vicegerents on earth, giving them all the abilities, values, and resources they need to live glorious lives and help others reach their greatest potential.

> *"It is He who hath made you (His) agents, inheritors of the earth: He hath raised you in ranks, some above others: that He may try you in the gifts He hath given you: for thy Lord is quick in punishment: yet He is indeed Oft-forgiving, Most Merciful. (Quran 6:165)*

Humans are endowed with extraordinary abilities and attributes that, when used appropriately, can lead to the accomplishment of miraculous objectives since they are representatives of Allah (SWT) Himself. However, to achieve these objectives, one must adhere to a set of guidelines and resources known as leadership principles.

As the vicegerent of Allah (SWT), humanity stands in for Him in the responsibility of understanding, communicating, and carrying out the laws of Allah (SWT) as leaders at all levels: on the level of the individual, family, community, or state, and in other spheres of life. Leadership concerns have been discussed throughout the Quran and the Sunnah in various ways, either emphasising its tenets or its illustrations. Eleven times in the Quran and innumerable times in the Sunnah, the word Imam, meaning leader in its various forms, including Imam, Imaman, Imamihim, and A'immah, is referenced.

Let's examine the few fundamental tenets of leadership in Islamic teachings. The first is "faith." Allah (SWT) affirms that people with faith and knowledge will experience perfection, superiority, and supremacy. Knowledge will enable people to identify the most efficient and effective way to carry out the impulse to do good, while faith will motivate them to do good to please Allah (SWT). In other words, Muslims are taught to uphold moral principles by their faith. People will become decent people and exhibit goodness if they have faith and knowledge. Therefore, it makes sense why knowledge and faith provide brilliance and greatness.

> *"O ye who believe, when ye are told to make room in the assemblies, (spread out and) make room: (ample) room will Allah provide for you. And when ye are told to rise up, rise up Allah will rise up, to (suitable) ranks (and degrees), those of you who believe and who have been granted (mystic) Knowledge. And Allah is well-acquainted with all ye do" (Quran 58:11)*

The second is "taqwa," which holds that every person or self is in charge of their own life. Everyone is in charge of their pleasure. Additionally, the recipient's self is a prize for their actions. Self-leadership, also known as personal leadership, is the cornerstone upon which all other forms of leadership must be based. Everyone must practise and uphold this leadership style, especially those in authority over the populace.

A true leader always focuses all his acts on Allah (SWT), expecting His favour and praying only for His reward. His emotions, words, and movements are always connected to the recollection of Allah (SWT), which is evidence that everything is worthy of devotion.

The first step in personal leadership is for leaders to decide on their aims or directions (AlIttijah). Stated differently, a leader needs to create a feeling of purpose in life. Then, it may be said that leadership is a journey with a destination; it's important to remember its precise objective. The greatest objective in life is the highest one that people can achieve.

Therefore, a person with vision, mentality, and character conducts himself well and lives purposefully. These are created and linked together. If a person's life vision is reflected in his character, that person is seen as genuinely honest. For instance, a student who claims to be anti-corruption but frequently takes books without intending to return them (or even loses them), uses his roommate's things without permission, and cheats on tests. His perception of corruption is undoubtedly confined to his imagination.

People who follow the proper principles (found in the Al-Quran) are undoubtedly cautious in their lives. Additionally, taqwa manifests itself in prudence. The devout person maintains the conviction that he is constantly watchful throughout his life's journey. As a result, the Quran becomes the guide that leads him to his ultimate objective in life.

> His perspective on the Quran is as follows, via Ibn al-Qayyim Al-Jauziyah: *Allah sent down the Quran for us to reflect on, we study it as a guide, we remember it as an entertainer, we interpret it in the best form and understanding, we believe, and we enforce its commands and prohibitions as much as possible. We can reap the fruit of useful knowledge that will lead us to Allah SWT from the trees and the garden of wisdom, both from the plants and flowers. Because the Quran is the book of*

Allah SWT that will show everything about Allah SWT for anyone who wants to know Him!

The Quran is Allah's (SWT) mercy given to us for the benefit of all living things, and the bright light of Allah (SWT) will drive out the darkness. When all other connections between Allah (SWT) and His slaves are severed, the Quran serves as a bridge. When all other gates are closed, we can reach Allah (SWT) through the Quran, the primary connection.

Important traits Muslim youth should cultivate:

Integrity and Trustworthiness: Maintaining the highest moral standards and exhibiting dependability are crucial in Islamic leadership. Strong moral principles underpin the decisions and actions of Islamic leaders, who behave with justice, honesty, and integrity. By continuously acting morally, they gain the respect and confidence of their followers and create a trusting atmosphere.

The importance of these traits in Islamic leadership is further supported by the emphasis on reliability exhibited by the Prophet Muhammad (PBUH). Islamic leaders inspire others by exhibiting integrity and dependability, encouraging responsibility, fostering positive work environments, and achieving common objectives—all of which eventually contribute to the development and prosperity of their communities.

Honesty and Truthfulness: Sincerity and truthfulness, rooted in Islamic beliefs, are valued highly by Islamic leadership. Leaders who promote clarity and trust exhibit these qualities. They lead with sincerity and communicate openly and truthfully, aiming to improve the lives of their followers and the community.

Integrity is essential because leaders maintain moral principles, are trustworthy, and carry out their duties. These attributes, including gaining respect and trust, are exemplified by Prophet Muhammad (PBUH). Islamic leaders offer a good example by upholding their moral duties. These attributes encourage openness, sincerity, and integrity and are fundamental to successful Islamic leadership.

Justice and Fairness: Islamic leadership highly values justice and equity, directing leaders to treat people fairly and give them equal chances regardless of their background or connections. Leaders must avoid nepotism and favouritism and base their judgements on merit and objective standards.

Leaders foster an inclusive atmosphere where everyone feels appreciated and has an equal opportunity to achieve by enforcing justice and fairness. These ideas are consistent with Islamic beliefs, which emphasise the value of fairness and treating everyone equally. Islamic leaders emphasise every person's intrinsic value and potential, encouraging harmony, cooperation, and togetherness within their group or community.

Humility and Modesty: Islamic leaders emphasise humility because they understand how important it is to value the contributions of others and foster an inclusive atmosphere. Islamic leaders know that genuine leadership is about helping others and fostering group development rather than vying for attention or establishing dominance. They demonstrate humility by recognising their shortcomings and limits, treating others with dignity and respect, and valuing different viewpoints and skills.

This modest approach fosters an atmosphere of equality and inclusivity, allowing people to feel appreciated and encouraged to give their all. Islamic leaders encourage trust, collaboration, and unity among their followers by modelling humility, which allows everyone to work together to accomplish common objectives.

Compassion and Empathy: Islamic leaders truly care about the welfare of their people and place a high value on empathy and compassion. They prioritise active listening and understanding to establish a welcoming and inclusive atmosphere where people feel appreciated, respected, and understood.

Islamic leaders constantly seek to lessen the physical and mental suffering of others and encourage a sense of camaraderie and brotherhood among their adherents. By exhibiting these traits, leaders encourage compassion and thoughtfulness, which promotes individual development and teamwork for the general welfare of the community.

Wisdom and Sound Judgment: Islamic leaders understand the need to make well-informed decisions, take long-term effects into account, and seek counsel as needed. Respected is the consultation concept (shūrā), which encourages shared accountability and a range of viewpoints. Islamic authorities welcome education and flexibility while staying receptive to criticism. They place a high value on accountable and capable leadership by making morally right decisions that advance society.

These attributes guide Muslim youth and foster wisdom, compassion, justice, and trust. Muslim youth leaders model these traits and encourage people to make constructive contributions to society.

Prophetic Qualities to Emulate in Youth Leadership

For all Muslim leaders, the Prophet Muhammad's (PBUH) leadership is the ultimate example. His character attributes have influenced the Islamic ummah's moral compass and still motivate leaders today. It's necessary to intentionally cultivate specific prophetic traits in Muslim youngsters before they assume leadership positions. The following are some of his most notable traits and life experiences that offer insightful leadership lessons:

Prophet Muhammad (PBUH) was referred to as "Al-Amīn" (the Trustworthy) because of his unwavering honesty and reliability. His community respected and trusted him even before he was given supernatural knowledge. He upheld high moral standards, kept his word, and arbitrated conflicts amicably. His excellent moral character is recognised by the Quran. The Prophet's integrity is a potent model for leaders, highlighting the significance of sincerity, honesty, and openness in leadership to win people over and create a climate of credibility and moral behaviour.

Prophet Muhammad (PBUH) actively sought the advice and opinions of his companions because he believed in consultative leadership. By including others in decision-making, he acknowledged the empowerment and advantages of many viewpoints and promoted unity, cooperation, and ownership within the Muslim community.

In Surah Al-'Imran (3:159), the Quran highlights consultative leadership, emphasising the Prophet's inclusive and gentle attitude. The passage emphasises the value of seeking advice from others and respecting their viewpoints to promote harmony. Modern leaders can learn from Prophet Muhammad's (PBUH) consultative leadership style, which encourages inclusivity and candid communication. Including a range of opinions in decision-making improves results and fosters a feeling of collective accountability. This strategy promotes harmony, cooperation, and a more robust group or community.

Prophet Muhammad (PBUH) showed extraordinary empathy and compassion for everyone, regardless of social standing. He comprehended viewpoints, actively listened, and offered direction and assistance. His empathy fostered a welcoming atmosphere where everyone felt appreciated and taken care of.

Anas ibn Malik gives an example that demonstrates the Prophet's kind and understanding demeanour. Out of compassion, he addressed the concerns of the underprivileged and disenfranchised in the larger community. This illustration emphasises how crucial empathy and compassion are to Islamic leadership, promoting a feeling of community and general well-being (Sahih Muslim).

Justice and equity were important to Prophet Muhammad (PBUH), who lived according to these ideals. He treated everyone equally, irrespective of their social standing or religious convictions. As a judge, he ensured just decisions based on Islamic law and the available facts.

He fought for the rights of the oppressed and questioned traditional norms to create a just social order.

The hadith in Sahih al-Bukhari highlights the Prophet's (PBUH) focus on honesty and reliability as necessary qualities. Today's leaders are motivated by the Prophet's (PBUH) dedication to justice, which preserves rights, promotes equality, and builds an inclusive society. Leaders who uphold justice cultivate a sense of worth and dignity, enhancing the community's general harmony and well-being.

Prophet Muhammad (PBUH) made wise decisions by seeking divine direction and considering long-term effects. He made decisions in accordance with Islamic beliefs because he recognised the consequences of his actions. He sought the wisdom of Allah (SWT) and made decisions based on revelations from the Almighty.

Quran 10:108 stresses the need to seek divine guidance and the Prophet's (PBUH) function as a guide. Leaders can learn from this example to think things through carefully, get advice, and make choices consistent with their beliefs. Leaders may learn a lot from these traits and examples from the life of the Prophet Muhammad (PBUH). Leaders can inspire and positively impact their communities by exhibiting integrity, compassion, justice, and knowledge. This creates an atmosphere that is inclusive, trusting, and conducive to progress.

Prophet Muhammad (PBUH) set an example by being patient, forgiving, humble, and thankful. His behaviour served as an example for his friends and still motivates people today. He maintained his humility, showed kindness to everyone, prioritised forgiveness over retaliation, showed patience when faced with difficulties, and conveyed thanks for his benefits. These attributes are modelled by the Prophet (PBUH), who inspires leaders to lead with compassion and honesty and creates circumstances conducive to progress (Sahih al- Bukhari).

Importance of Self-awareness and Personal Development

Self-awareness involves the ability to objectively recognise and understand one's own feelings, strengths, shortcomings, and ideals. It's essential for effective leadership and a fundamental component of both professional and personal growth. Self-awareness influences one's behaviour and interactions with others, enabling one to assess and modify one's leadership style as needed.

In the Quran, Allah (SWT) says: "And be not like those who forgot Allah (SWT), so He made them forget themselves" (59:19). Forgetting one's purpose leads to an identity crisis, while remembering Allah (SWT) brings clarity, direction, and self-knowledge. Umar ibn Al-Khattab advised, "Take account of yourselves before you are taken to account." When young leaders engage in honest introspection, they become more effective leaders, more conscious of their impact, and more aligned with Islamic ethics.

Establishing a strong awareness of oneself becomes even more important in today's fast-paced society, where young people are continuously inundated with information and diversions.

Being self-aware is similar to having a compass that points you toward what is true to who you are. It allows you to make decisions fundamentally consistent with who you are. By adopting self-awareness as a crucial tool for personal development, young individuals can reach their full potential and confidently negotiate life's curveballs.

Self-aware young leaders can properly regulate their emotions so that they don't affect their judgment or ability to make decisions. Leaders must remain composed and make objective decisions in fast-paced, often stressful situations.

As Allah (SWT) makes abundantly evident in the Holy Quran, humans are the best of the creation. We are superior to all other creations because of the wisdom Allah (SWT), our Creator, has given us. Everybody has ideas. Humans can reflect on their current condition and assess various scenarios. Self-awareness allows us to monitor our thinking and, in turn, gives us insight into our intentions and motives.

For instance, every idea that enters our minds originates from somewhere. Most often than not, we're preoccupied with thoughts about our everyday routines or social interactions. If a colleague treats us rudely, we might dwell on it for the rest of the day. It's pretty easy for our minds to spiral into negative thinking. When we practice self-awareness, we can interrupt that vicious loop and break it.

Self-awareness involves three important steps: It starts with admitting that your opinion of yourself does not match that of others. Most leaders lack perception, listing items as strengths that others might consider faults. On the other hand, many people have hidden strengths—things others perceive but do not.

Second, it entails sorting through the comments you get to determine what is important enough to take action on. Accepting criticism might be contradictory and isn't always pertinent to your development, even if it's essential for understanding how others see you. Asking yourself, "How does this feedback relate to the individual I want to be, how I want to act, and how I want to show up for my people?" will help you consider the special contribution you hope to make as a leader. Whose and what feedback am I missing?

Third, adopting this mindset necessitates considering the effects of your words and actions on other people and making necessary adjustments. It's the idea that your impact and contribution directly relate to your capacity to learn more about yourself. This entails continuous learning, developing, recognising the effects, and modifying. When you can identify how your mindful leadership affects other people, you may use that understanding to improve relationships and your leadership. Since awareness of impact is based on reciprocity and trust, it necessitates checking in with people and communicating.

Including self-awareness in leadership practice is a path of constant improvement rather than a quick fix. By participating in this process, young leaders can significantly increase their efficacy, which will have a good knock-on effect. Leaders may become more strategic, inspirational, and empathic by identifying their strengths and opportunities for growth through self-evaluation, observation, and candid feedback. A leader who understands their reactions, manages stress, and acts with wisdom embodies the prophetic approach.

Developing Leadership Skills through Continuous Improvement

Effective leadership is dynamic. It's an energetic process that benefits greatly from growth, curiosity, and adaptation. Great leaders are lifelong learners. They know how important it is to be knowledgeable and flexible in ever-changing environments. Our Prophet Muhammad (PBUH) also stressed the value of education and knowledge. He urged his disciples to pursue knowledge in all fields, religious and secular, and to always aim for intellectual and personal development.

This lesson reminds us of the value of lifelong learning and intellectual curiosity in today's fast-paced, constantly evolving world. During his mission, he also developed his own intelligence and tactics. The same attitude should be adopted by upcoming Muslim leaders: a never-ending quest for progress via introspection, research, mentoring, and action.

Young leaders need to understand the significant influence of ongoing development on their leadership development. Effective leadership is largely shaped by continuous development, not just a professional duty. It's impossible to overestimate the importance of ongoing leadership development. Leaders with a continuous improvement approach can better recognise and address new issues as they arise.

A proactive attitude is fostered by continuous development, which enables leaders to foresee changes and come up with creative answers in advance. Leaders who put their own development first can better encourage and inspire their colleagues, resulting in increased engagement and output. A dedication to ongoing development also shows an investment in one's future. It broadens their viewpoints and improves decision-making skills, preparing leaders for more challenging tasks and larger responsibilities. Leaders create a strong foundation for long-term success by continuously improving their abilities and competencies. Self-reflection allows a leader to examine what worked, what didn't, and why. It's a tool for learning from failure without being defined by it.

> *The Prophet (PBUH) said: "The strong believer is better and more beloved to Allah than the weak believer, while there is good in both. Be eager for what benefits you. Seek help from Allah and do not give up" (Sahih Muslim)*

Growth-oriented leadership draws strength from perseverance and a desire to be better for the sake of Allah (SWT).

Continuous improvement requires humility and effort. A youth leader must actively pursue knowledge—Islamic knowledge, interpersonal skills, management strategies, and more. Every experience becomes an opportunity to grow closer to Allah (SWT) and become more capable of serving others.

Leadership in Islam is a journey of the soul as much as of action. It begins with sincerity, grows with self-awareness, and blossoms through service to others. For the Muslim youth, becoming a leader means aligning one's heart with the Quran, character with the Prophet (PBUH), and purpose with the call to serve humanity with truth, justice, and compassion.

Chapter Four

Inspirational Examples of Youth Leadership in Islamic History

Profiles of Young Leaders from Islamic History

Numerous leaders have existed throughout human history. Some of these figures were selected as leaders due to their exceptional traits, but many others attained leadership by force or heredity. Some leaders from the latter category have also come to prominence, whose contributions to humanity transcend time and location; their lives, creations, and quotes serve as a source of inspiration and motivation for future generations.

Visionary and moral leadership have brought the Ummah together, advancing justice and bringing about wealth throughout Islamic history. Great Islamic young leaders follow the example of our Prophet Muhammad (PBUH), the Rightly Guided Caliphs (Al-Khulafa Ar-Rashidun) and many others guided by the principles of the Quran and the Sunnah. This, in turn, shaped the services they provided to the communities; they were based on justice, compassion, and obedience to Allah (SWT). Given the numerous difficulties the Muslim world faces, we must look to the leadership of the past for guidance in the present and the future.

The legacy of Islam is rich with stories of young individuals who rose to prominence not through wealth or age but through their character, courage, and unshakable faith. Their stories inspire generations of Muslims seeking to serve with integrity and excellence. Let's have a look at a few of them:

Ali ibn Abi Talib (RA)

Ali ibn Abi Talib (RA), the first Imam (leader) and the fourth Rashidun caliph, who reigned from 656 CE to 661, is among the most prominent. He was the Holy Prophet's (PBUH) son-in-law and cousin. Because they both had a grandpa named Abdul-Mutalib ibn Hakim, Muslims acknowledge him as the first person to convert to Islam and as Prophet Mohammed's paternal cousin.

He is well-known among Muslims for his bravery, moral integrity, simplicity, and role as a representation of justice and equity. One might see how he accepted important leadership qualities while in power by taking a snapshot of his life. Ali (RA) implemented significant adjustments to monetary and fiscal policies that upheld the ideas of fairness and equality for all. Although his caliphate lasted from 656 to 661, Shia Muslims consider Ali (RA) to be the Prophet Muhammad's (PBUH) legitimate immediate successor, or "Imam."

During the time of the Prophet Muhammad (PBUH), Imam Ali (AS) was the victor of numerous battles. He participated in every war and campaign except the one to Tabuk, where he was supposed to represent the Prophet Muhammad (PBUH) in Medina. During his lifetime, no one was ever permitted to impersonate the Prophet Muhammad (PBUH) in his hometown in any way. Imam Ali is revered for his vast understanding of Arabic literature and grammar, Islamic law, astronomy, and theology and his reputation as a righteous leader. In 658 AD, he wrote a historic letter to Malik Al-Ashtar, the newly appointed governor of Egypt, outlining his policies and governing principles. He ruled justly and modestly as the fourth caliph. His early deeds set the stage for his subsequent leadership and demonstrated that, when led by integrity and morality, youth need not hinder greatness.

Mus'ab ibn Umair (RA)

Mus'ab ibn Umair (RA), a young Meccan nobleman who converted to Islam against the wishes of his affluent family, is another compelling example. Growing up, Mus'ab ibn Umair (RA) was surrounded by wealth and splendour. His wealthy parents gave him a lot of care and attention. Mus'ab (RA), who was once renowned for his status and elegance, gave up his comforts for Allah (SWT).

He was appointed by the Prophet (PBUH) as the first Islamic ambassador to Yathrib (later Madinah), where he spread the faith and laid the foundation for the Prophet's (PBUH) journey. His insight and ability to communicate brought the people of Madinah together around a common religion. Despite his early death at the Battle of Uhud, Mus'ab will always be remembered as a pioneering young leader.

Usama ibn Zayd (RA)

Usama ibn Zayd (RA) is another great young leader of Islamic history. Despite being only seventeen, he was appointed by the Prophet (PBUH) to lead a military expedition that included veteran companions. This decision shocked many, but the Prophet (PBUH) affirmed his leadership based on merit and not age: "If you question his leadership now, you questioned his father's leadership before, and he was worthy of it. Indeed, he [Usama] is worthy of leadership." Usama's (RA) appointment teaches that youth should not be dismissed due to age if they display competence and character.

Zayd ibn Harithah (RA) and the Prophet Muhammad (PBUH) shared a remarkable tie based on righteousness, love, and trust. According to Hazrat Aisha (RA), the Prophet (PBUH) rushed to greet Zayd (RA) and give him a forehead kiss when he knocked on his door after a journey. Zayd's (RA) strong ties to the Prophet (PBUH) were also evident in his command of the troops. Zayd (RA), a former slave, was trusted to command the Muslim army in a number of significant conflicts, including the Battle of Mu'tah and in this battle, he was martyred.

Moreover, we may learn a lot from Prophet Muhammad's (PBUH) life and, more significantly, his leadership of the Ummah. Exemplary leadership was demonstrated by the Prophet (PBUH) and his Companions. These stories offer timeless lessons. The companions demonstrated that youth leadership is not about status or personal gain but service, sacrifice, and vision. They placed the mission of Islam above their desires and endured hardship with patience. To be an effective leader, we must be accountable and develop a number of virtues. The Sunnah teaches us the following leadership lessons:

> *Abdullah ibn Umar (RA) reported that the Messenger of Allah (PBUH) said: "Each of you is a shepherd, and each of you is responsible for his flock. A leader is a shepherd over his people, and he is responsible for his flock. A man is a shepherd over the members of his household, and he is responsible for his flock. A servant is a shepherd over his master's wealth, and he is responsible for it. Each of you is a shepherd, and each of you is responsible for his flock."(Al-Adab al-Mufrad by Imam al-Bukhari)*

This hadith teaches us the value of responsibility. Whether a manager taking care of an employee or a parent taking care of a child, we must recognise our leadership positions in life and ensure that anyone we are responsible for is taken care of effectively. It's part of the Sunnah to be accountable.

Muslims are cautioned against assuming positions of authority or dominating others. We are told to lead for the proper reasons and to keep Allah (SWT) in mind at all times. The Prophet Muhammad (PBUH) said:

> *"O Abdur-Rahman! Do not ask for a position of leadership, for if you receive it as a result of asking, you will be left alone with it, and if you receive it without asking, you will be aided in it" (Tirmidhi)*

Our status can be improved by whatever good deeds we undertake to assume the responsibilities of a leadership role. However, it is against the Prophet's (PBUH) Sunnah if we consciously aim to rise to positions of leadership to earn notoriety or to exert control over others.

Prophet Muhammad (PBUH) and his companions were exceptional leaders in part because of their outstanding moral integrity. Many leaders nowadays succumb to conceit, the carelessness of their subordinates, or control-freak tendencies. Abdullah ibn Amr (RA) reported that the Messenger of Allah (PBUH was neither harsh nor rude in speech. He was never loud or boisterous in the marketplace. The Prophet (PBUH) would say:

> *The best of you are those who have the best character"* (Sahih al-Bukhari)

Leadership styles of the first four Caliphs

Following the death of the Prophet Muhammad, the early Islamic period is a foundational era in Islamic history. This period saw the rise of the first four Caliphs, often referred to as the "Rightly Guided Caliphs." These leaders played crucial roles in the Islamic state's expansion and consolidation, while laying the groundwork for future governance. Each of the early Islamic leaders brought their unique approach to leadership, which not only helped stabilise the newly formed Islamic state but also left an enduring legacy for future generations. Understanding their strategies and principles allows modern leaders to better appreciate the values and methodologies contributing to their success.

First Caliph: Hazrat Abu Bakr (RA)

Following the passing of the Prophet Muhammad (PBUH), Abu Bakr became the first Caliph of Islam. He is one of the higher members of the Quraysh tribe in Mecca. Muhammad changed his name to Abu Bakr once he converted to Islam. Ash-Shiddiq, which translates to "trusted one," was his given name. He is regarded as one of Muhammad's (PBUH) closest and most devoted friends, standing up for Muslims even while his own people were attacking them. The social, cultural, and law enforcement facets of Arab society under Islam advanced quickly during the two years Abu Bakr (RA) presided over it. Abu Bakr (RA) also oversaw the conquest of parts of the Byzantine Empire and the expansion of Islamic territory into Persia and the Arabian Peninsula.

Throughout his life, Abu Bakr (RA) made numerous contributions to Islam. It took a lot of courage for him. Even though there were only 38 Muslims, he spread the word about Islam to non-believers. He consistently encouraged the Prophet Muhammad (PBUH) to publicly preach Islam.

He was the first Muslim in his country to preach a sermon urging people to follow Allah. He was nearly slain when the Quraish people became outraged after he publicly delivered lessons. His top priority when he regained consciousness was to ensure Prophet Muhammad's (PBUH) safety. His devotion to Prophet Muhammad (PBUH) surpasses his devotion to his family and life.

A remarkable example of leadership, Abu Bakr al-Siddiq (RA) was wise and perceptive in his use of justice, consultation, and efficient national communication. Although difficult, these made it feasible to manage crises and bring tribes together. He established an Islamic state that existed, developed, and spread in a manner that would not have been possible without his careful and creative leadership.

Second Caliph: Hazrat Umar ibn al-Khattab (RA)

After conferring with the senior Sahaba before his passing, Sayyiduna Abu Bakr (RA) appointed Sayyiduna Umar (RA) as the second Caliph of the Muslims. "Al Farooq," or "One who distinguishes between Right and Wrong," is how Islamic tradition refers to Umar (RA), Khattab's son. Umar's (RA) reign was characterised by the growth of the Muslim empire and equitable governance; his emphasis on justice and administrative improvements enabled him to strike a balance between religious values and efficient rule. Islam flourished quickly during Umar's (RA) rule, and there was conflict with neighbouring territories.

The majority of the population, however, felt free and content to welcome Muslim leaders in place of the previous despicable and dishonest ones. Umar (RA) was recognised as the greatest judge during his reign, and both Sunni and Shi'i legal scholars hold his rulings in the highest regard. Umar's (RA) strong administration and decisiveness were hallmarks of his leadership. He greatly enlarged the Islamic state. Umar (RA) established a successful judicial administration system.

The administration of justice was based on Islamic precepts. Judges, or qadis, were appointed at all levels of government. The first king in history to divide the executive and judicial branches was Umar (RA). The leadership of Umar ibn al-Khattab (RA) was distinguished by his deep commitment to justice, effective management, and the well-being of his subjects. His accomplishments and contributions established fundamental guidelines for the Islamic state's future expansion and advancement.

Third Caliph: Hazrat Uthman ibn Affan (RA)

Sayyiduna Umar (RA) established a six-member committee to choose his successor from among them prior to his death. After extensive deliberation and consultation, they chose Sayyiduna 'Uthman bin Affan (RA) as the third Caliph of Islam. Sayyiduna 'Uthman (RA) was a member of the Quraish Ummayah tribe. He was a fabric merchant of great wealth. He was called "The Generous" or "Al Ghani." His mother was Urwa, and his father was Affan.

Centralisation of authority and standardisation of religious writings (the Quran) were hallmarks of Uthman's (RA) reign. We know Uthman (RA) for his contribution to the history of the religion: penning down the Quran. During Uthman's (RA) rule, infrastructure and the economy both expanded. Zakat, Khara, Jazya, Ushr, Fay, and Ghanimah were the state's financial resources at the time.

They significantly raised the state's income or earnings during this time, which was characterised by the quick expansion of Islamic territory as an indication of sound government. In Muslim communities, the aforementioned financial resources are still acknowledged. The idea of servant leadership is demonstrated by Uthman's (RA) readiness to help the community and meet its needs. Leaders ought to put their followers' well-being first and be prepared to give up something personal to further the common good.

The effects of Uthman's (RA) rule were long-lasting in terms of politics, economy, and religion. He reorganised caliphal regions, or junds, which were sometimes modelled after Byzantine provincial divisions, and revitalised the administrative frameworks of his provinces. Economic reforms were also introduced by Uthman (RA). Among the most noteworthy were striking new coins that featured Arabic, including dirhams of the Sasanian type that read "Bismallah," which translates to "In the name of Allah."

The Quran's recension, an attempt to preserve a common understanding of the divine word by editing disparate textual traditions, is Uthman's (RA) most enduring contribution. He ordered canonical copies to be sent to Damascus, Mecca, Basra, and Kufa and formed a commission to discuss these differences. He gave the order to destroy older Quranic versions. The people of his era admired and revered him because of his kindness, which also improved the conditions for Muslims.

Fourth Caliph: Hazrat Ali (RA)

The fourth Caliph of Islam, Ali ibn Abi Talib (RA), came to power amid great difficulty and internal conflict. Despite strong opposition and turmoil during his rule, he showed determination and fortitude in leading the Muslim community. His leadership style was marked by resistance and justice.

He was renowned for his dedication to maintaining moral purity and his keen sense of fairness. Ali (RA) understood the value of transparency and accountability in government. As a result, Ali (RA) emphasised that every leader must guarantee that everyone under their control is treated fairly. Because of this, he could steer clear of favouritism and nepotism in his leadership.

Ali (RA) showed tremendous bravery, tenacity, and fortitude while serving as a leader. During his reign as Caliph, he had many difficulties and crises, such as political disputes and military confrontations, yet he persisted. The current leaders should learn from this to be resilient in leadership challenges and to look for ways to get past political obstacles that stand in the way of preserving peace and stability in their leadership.

Authoritarian, democratic or participative, and delegating are the three types of leadership. With no input or guidance, autocratic leaders dictate to their followers what they must do and how to do it. When decision-making is required in a democratic or participatory setting, the leader enlists the help of one or more employees. However, the leader typically makes all of the decisions and retains the final decision that is carried out, which establishes the leader's power. Although employees make decisions when delegated, the leader is still held accountable and liable for the choices made.

There is a correlation between the four first Caliphs' leadership styles and the aforementioned leadership philosophies. A small number of Caliphs advocated for participatory or democratic leadership. For instance, they formed a team to vote for the Caliph during the selection. The public was given the chance to take part in an election. Democracy is this. Among the Caliphs who supported democracy was Umar (RA). The Caliphs occasionally choose the empire's ruler without seeking input from others, as was the case with Abu Bakr's (RA) decision to lead the war of apostasy.

'Uthman (RA) did not consult his people before choosing to give preference to his kin. These are instances of autocratic leadership. By selecting the governors of various regions, the Caliphs further encouraged the delegation of leadership. Ali (RA) and Uthman (RA) did this. They were held liable and accountable for the choices made by those governors.

Impactful Contributions of Young Muslim Leaders in Various Fields

Islamic history is also filled with brilliant young minds who made lasting contributions beyond the battlefield or mosque. These individuals influenced the sciences, governance, scholarship, and social reform, proving that youth are not just the future, but often the force of change in the present.

Imam al-Shafi'i, one of the four great imams of Islamic jurisprudence, memorised the Quran by age seven and began issuing legal rulings in his early twenties. His contributions to Islamic legal methodology shaped the development of fiqh across the Muslim world. His intellect was sharpened by early exposure to knowledge and a sincere pursuit of truth.

Muhammad al-Fatih, also known as Sultan Mehmed II, conquered Constantinople at the age of twenty-one, fulfilling a prophecy of the Prophet Muhammad (PBUH):

> *"Verily, you shall conquer Constantinople. What a wonderful leader will her leader be, and what a wonderful army will that army be" (Musnad Ahmad)*

This young ruler combined military genius with religious conviction, ushering in a new era of Islamic influence. His leadership was marked by discipline, strategy, and deep commitment to Islam.

Fatimah al-Fihri, though not commonly highlighted, made a profound impact as a young woman who founded the University of Al-Qarawiyyin in Morocco during the 9th century. Recognised by UNESCO as the oldest existing and continually operating educational institution in the world, her initiative shows how young Muslims, regardless of gender, have shaped knowledge and civilisation.

Modern Muslim youth can reclaim their sense of purpose by reflecting on the lives of remarkable young figures in Islam's history. Leadership is not easy but rewarding—especially when rooted in sincerity, humility, and faith. The leaders of yesterday rose because they knew who they were, who they served, and why they were called to act. The youth of today must do the same.

Chapter Five

Youth Leadership in the Quran and Sunnah

Quranic Narratives of Youth Leadership

Learning from the Quran is a dynamic process and a constant source of guidance. One of the many ways the Quran teaches us is through the accounts of prophets, monarchs, and regular people. Once more, these stories can teach different lessons to different people in different situations and times.

The Quran offers a rich tapestry of tales that emphasise the importance of young people in leadership roles and serving God. These stories are timeless illustrations of how young people may lead with courage, wisdom, and conviction when firmly rooted in their faith and directed by moral principles.

Story of Dhul-Qarnayn

Surah Kahf (Surah 18) of the Quran tells the tale of Dhul Qarnayn. Unbelievers allegedly attempted to test the Prophet Muhammad (PBUH) by asking Muslims to pose questions to him that they believed he would not be able to respond to, unless he were the Prophet (PBUH). They then questioned him about souls, a man travelling around, and several young people living in caves. At this time, Allah (SWT) revealed the solutions to these queries to the Prophet (PBUH) in the Revelation of Surah Kahf.

> *The Quran says: "They ask you concerning Zul-qarnain. Say "I will rehearse to you something of his story" (18:83)*

> *Then, it says: "Verily We established his power on earth and We gave him the ways and the means to all ends." (Quran 18:84)*

In the Dhul Qarnayn narrative, we are reminded that Allah (SWT) is the Sovereign. He gives us varying degrees of authority, assigns us tasks, and uses us to carry out His will. However, he will not insist that we complete a task without providing the necessary tools. According to Allah (SWT), he created Dhul Qarnayn on earth and provided him with all the resources, skills, and means necessary for everything.

The other side of this is that Allah (SWT) doesn't ask us to perform anything that we are incapable of doing. Humanly speaking, this means that when we are in a leadership role, we should expect the best of the people we assign tasks to, but only if we give them the tools and training they need to complete the work, and we don't expect more than we know they can deliver.

Being a leader is not exploitative. When Dhul Qarnayn encounters someone who is unfamiliar to him and speaks a different language, he treats them with service rather than greed. They even offer to pay for him to build a barrier to keep out foreign attackers, but Dhul Qarnayn doesn't ask for more or even take what is offered to him voluntarily, since he doesn't want to take advantage of their vulnerability. He would expect something from them if they fought him and lost, but not when they essentially gave up and showed him their frailty.

He is therefore giving, just like a good leader. He also maintains his humility in his charity since he acknowledges that Allah (SWT) is the source of everything he possesses. Additionally, he understands that the power bestowed upon him by Allah (SWT) is merely a tool for serving Allah (SWT). He fulfils his role as a servant-leader by attending to the needs of his people.

Being a leader is a continuous challenge. Dhul Qarnayn was put to test. After gaining power and the ability to do anything, he is now asked to make decisions regarding a group of people that he has seemingly overrun. He demonstrates the insight of a wise leader by differentiating between the virtuous and the unrighteous. He demonstrates the virtues of justice and fairness as a leader. Good people must be rewarded and honoured, while bad people must be punished. Take note of the two phases in every instance.

Since leaders cannot do anything without their followers—and of course, Allah's (SWT) assistance—leadership is about teamwork. After stating that what he has from Allah (SWT) is superior to what they can provide, Dhul Qarnayn offers to assist them if they cooperate with him and work as a team. This action accomplishes the three goals of effective leadership: (1) asking for the people's assistance elevates them as partners in the problem-solving process; (2) it gives them a stake in the solution's success; and (3) it instills in them a sense of accountability for taking ownership of and upholding the solution they have developed. It's also crucial to remember that he wants them to use their strengths, which are what they do have.

Thus, the story of Dhul-Qarnayn teaches that true leadership is rooted in humility, justice, and service to others. It reminds us that with every responsibility comes the necessary support from Allah (SWT) to fulfil it. Ultimately, a righteous leader uplifts others by guiding them with fairness and empowering them through collaboration.

Story of Prophet Yusuf (Joseph) (PBUH)

The story of Prophet Yusuf (Joseph) (PBUH) is among the most potent. When he was younger, Yusuf showed great patience, emotional intelligence, and faith in Allah (SWT). Ten half-brothers were born to Prophet Yusuf, son of Yacoub (Jacob). According to reports, Yusuf was his father's favourite son, which made his brothers envious. When Yusuf was seventeen, he had a dream in which Yacoub cautioned him not to tell his brothers if they tried to hurt him.

This suggested that Yusuf would eventually rise to a position of authority and that his father, mother, and brothers would even submit to him. His brothers chose to get rid of their younger brother because they were so envious. A gang of traders eventually discovered Yusuf in the well and sold him to the captain of the Egyptian Pharaoh's guard.

He eventually rose to the position of personal servant to the captain and then superintendent of his household. It was well known that Yusuf was extremely attractive, so Zuleika, the captain's wife, attempted to court him. Because of his fear of Allah (SWT) and his religion, Yusuf turned down her advances. She falsely accused him out of anger, which resulted in his incarceration.

Allah (SWT) gave Yusuf the gift of dream interpretation while he was incarcerated. Two other guys received prison sentences at about the same time. One served as the King's chef, and the other as a cupbearer. His religiosity captivated Yusuf's cellmates, who turned to him for explanations of their visions. The other dreamed that he was carrying food on his head while two birds were consuming it, while the first dreamed that he was serving the monarch a drink.

> *Yusuf (AS) initially called them to Allah (SWT), then interpreted, "O two companions of prison, as for one of you, he will give drink to his master of wine; but as for the other, he will be crucified, and the birds will eat*

> *from his head. The matter has been decreed about which you both inquire" (Quran 12:41). And he said to the one he knew would go free,"Mention me before the king."*
> *(Quran 12:42)*

However, Shaitan forced him to forget about [mentioning] his master and Yusuf (AS) spent several years behind bars. Nevertheless, he dedicated those years to remembering Allah (SWT) and made patience his own.

Despite being betrayed by his own brothers and sold into slavery, he rose through trials with steadfastness. In the palace of Egypt, when faced with temptation, he chose righteousness over desire, saying:

> *"I seek the refuge of Allah. Indeed, He is my Master, who has made good my residence. Indeed, wrongdoers will not succeed" (Surah Yusuf 12:23)*

Later, his leadership and wisdom during the famine saved an entire nation. His life exemplifies how youth can lead through integrity, patience, and a deep awareness of divine purpose.

Story of Prophet Ibrahim (Abraham) (PBUH)

Another striking example is Prophet Ibrahim (Abraham) (PBUH), who challenged his community's idol worship as a youth. In the ancient land of Babylonia (present-day Iraq), people worshipped their idols. They worshipped the deities they had fashioned by themselves from wood and stone. They might have found it simpler to worship something they had made up because they could choose between right and wrong thanks to the gods they had made themselves. Ibrahim was different from the other kids; he was not likely to succumb to their idolatry. He sought the truth, and his creator endowed him with intelligence.

Abraham developed over the years. His disdain for these idols has existed since he was a young boy. He found it incomprehensible that a rational person could create and revere a statue. He saw that these idols could not turn themselves right side up if turned upside down and did not eat, drink, or speak. So, how could anyone think that sculptures like that could be good or bad for them?

Abraham's people had a large temple filled with idols, with a niche in the centre that held the largest gods of all shapes, sizes, and attributes. As a child, Abraham often accompanied his father to the temple, and he hated all that stone and wood. He was taken aback by his people's behaviour when they entered the temple; they bowed and began to weep, pleading and pleading with their gods for assistance as though the idols could hear or comprehend them!

Abraham went to a mountain one night after leaving his home. He wandered by himself in the dark till he found a mountain cave and sat with his back to the wall. He looked at the sky. When he realised that he was staring at planets and stars that some people on Earth adored, he had barely noticed it. A great deal of grief flooded his little heart. He thought about what was beyond the moon, stars, and planets and was amazed that people worshipped these heavenly bodies when they were made to adore and follow their Creator, rising and falling at His command.

Now, Ibrahim needed to remind statue worshippers of their mistakes and point them in the correct direction. As a responsible son, Ibrahim decided to educate his father first. Ibrahim infuriated his father. He openly disputed their gods here, although he expected his kid to become a priest.

Undeterred by the hostility of his father and community, Ibrahim (PBUH) set out to demonstrate the futility of idol worship. One day, when the townspeople had gone to a festival outside the city, Ibrahim entered the temple alone. He shattered all the smaller idols with an axe, leaving the biggest one intact. He hung the axe around its neck, a symbolic gesture. When the people returned and were outraged, they questioned him. He pointed to the large idol and mockingly suggested they ask it what had happened.

The people realised the truth in his statement, for they knew the idol could not speak. Yet their arrogance and pride blinded them. Instead of admitting their error, they turned on Ibrahim. The king, Nimrod, ordered that Ibrahim be burned alive. A massive fire was prepared. But Allah (SWT) commanded the fire, "Be cool and safe for Ibrahim." To everyone's amazement, Ibrahim emerged unharmed. This miracle strengthened the faith of those who had begun to doubt the idols.

Eventually, Ibrahim left his people. He travelled to many lands, always preaching the oneness of Allah (SWT). He was blessed with righteous children, including Prophet Ismail (Ishmael) and Prophet Ishaq (Isaac), and his lineage became the root of great prophets. His legacy as the father of monotheism endures in Islam, Christianity, and Judaism.

In sum, Prophet Ibrahim's (PBUH) story teaches us to seek truth with courage and conviction. His unwavering stand against falsehood, even in youth, exemplifies true faith. He questioned what others blindly followed and turned instead to the Creator of the universe. His journey reminds us of the power of reflection and inner strength. Through integrity, patience, and a deep awareness of divine purpose, he became a guiding light for generations.

Analysing Leadership Values Exhibited by Believers in the Quran

Tawhid

The understanding of Allah's (SWT) unity and authority over life and livelihood is the foundation of Islamic leadership. "Tawhid" is the Islamic term for this central idea. It is the view that everything, including himself, his leadership, and everything under his direction, belongs to Allah (SWT) and is therefore subject to his will. Allah (SWT) created the universe and everything in it so people could worship Him.

Beginning with the goal of serving Allah (SWT), every choice, rule, and business operation within the company is always made to abide by Sharia law and must even have the value of worshipping and appeasing Allah (SWT). A leader can avoid becoming conceited and self-centred, which are the biggest enemies of effective leadership, by correctly comprehending and believing in the notion of tawhid, which acknowledges that all belongs to Allah (SWT).

Amanah

This idea has to do with having the capacity for responsibility. There are two perspectives on Amanah in leadership. The first is the amanah, which acknowledges that a leadership role is a gift from Allah (SWT) and that one will answer to Him for it. The second quality a leader needs to possess is amanah, which has to do with his reputation and capacity to uphold trust in front of his followers and other stakeholders, to whom he is also accountable.

Thus, from an Islamic standpoint, the authority to lead an organisation genuinely originates from Allah when that individual is chosen through an election process by the organisation's members. Thus, any behaviour that has the potential to harm the organisation and its members might be considered a violation of the Amanah. The people he leads will not sympathise with a leader who contradicts his actions with his words. The primary quality that the most successful leaders have in common is integrity.

Al-Birr

Al-Birr is a word for virtue or doing well. In Surat Al-Baqarah/2: 177, the Quran describes the broad definition of *ibadah* as virtuous actions. Islamic leadership includes the sincere desire to improve the lives of others, particularly those under the leader's supervision, as much as feasible.

To embody the value of birr in leadership, a leader must be sensitive to the spiritual, material, bodily, and psychological needs of those they lead. A leader guided by the principles of *birr* principles will be more focused on serving others, realising that his primary responsibility is to assist others under his direction in realising their full potential rather than putting in extra effort to be well-served.

Nadzhrah

Nadzhrah signifies vision or seeing. On the other hand, a visionary leader is someone who can create and develop a vision. The Prophet Muhammad's (PBUH) leadership role is closely associated with the visionary character. The Prophet's (PBUH) capacity to foresee the future inspired his followers. The individuals under a leader's direction look to him to provide them with a vision of the organisation's future.

The vision needs to be properly formulated and conveyed for the intended motivational effect to be realised. In a contemporary business setting, a vision created collaboratively through shura (the deliberation process) is thought to be more effective in igniting the organisation, even though the leader may construct it autocratically. Building a sense of unity, joy, and readiness to work together to accomplish organisational goals is one of the objectives of imparting a vision.

Mujahadah

Mujahadah can be seen as a sincere attitude, struggle, or striving. A leader must demonstrate their completeness in doing their leadership responsibilities. This is also connected to the last characteristic, itqon, where a leader can demonstrate their genuine enthusiasm and commitment to a field.

However, as the Prophet stated that the most significant jihad is war against oneself and lust, the primary and initial context of itqon is associated with the severity of leading oneself (spiritual struggle) to remain above the standard of truth and righteousness established by the leader. It's morally expected of a leader to become a role model, most respected for their aptitude, seriousness, passion, and work ethic.

A leader's responsibilities and challenges increase with their position. Therefore, a leader needs to have patience.

> *The Quran clearly links leadership with patience: "We raised from among them leaders, guiding by Our command, when they patiently endured and firmly believed in Our signs" (Quran 32:24)*

Adl

In the Islamic tradition, the word "leadership" is firmly associated with the adjective "adl," which means "fair." On the Day of Judgement (al-Qiyamah), Allah (SWT) will provide refuge to seven groups, including the just or fair leader. Adl literally means "to put something in its place," and being fair means being impartial without being swayed by subjective elements like one's own interests.

Because of their authority, a person in a leadership role is more susceptible to injustice. This may result in the misuse of authority. When a leader gives someone more money based on their proximity or preference rather than their ability and performance, that is an example of injustice in the workplace. Organisations will suffer from this since other employees will compare themselves to one another and feel this is unfair, lowering their motivation for their jobs.

Shura

Even while leaders must be experts in their domains, they do not have to be the most educated about every facet and area of their work before making judgments and acting on them. This relates to another principle called shura, which states that the leader must be able to use the discussion process to foster effective cooperation and a sense of community.

Decisions are made in shura through consultation with assembly members to arrive at a consensus, or mufakat. This shura can also realise other values and principles, such as justice ('adl), in which each assembly member's voice is respected and heard.

Amanah, a leader, realises that the organisation they lead is not solely their own when they recognise that their leadership authority is a mandate given to them by God through the people they lead. A leader may choose not to use the shura principles when making judgments for three reasons. First, self-interest causes others' voting rights to be disregarded. Second, the leader despises other people's skills and believes he is better than they are. Third, shura is unattainable due to an emergency that necessitates a quick judgment. From an Islamic standpoint, the first and second causes are vile attitudes, whereas only the third requirement is permitted.

The Quranic portrayals of young believers underscore a recurring theme: youth who lead with sincerity, courage, and unwavering faith. These individuals do not rely on status or age but on their connection with Allah (SWT), willingness to speak truth to power, and commitment to justice. Leadership in these narratives is not defined by control over others but by moral clarity, wisdom in adversity, and readiness to act for the greater good.

Guidance from the Sunnah on Nurturing Leadership Potential in Young Muslims

The Prophet Muhammad (PBUH) exemplified a nurturing leadership style. He corrected with gentleness, encouraged with love, and guided with wisdom. He saw the potential in each young person and created opportunities for them to grow.

He instructed young people to pray, to lead in community affairs, to ask questions, and to contribute ideas.

> *Anas ibn Malik, who served the Prophet from a young age, said: "I served the Messenger of Allah for ten years, and he never said to me, 'Uff,' and never said to me concerning anything I had done, 'Why did you do that?' nor concerning anything I had not done, 'Why did you not do that?'" (Bukhari)*

This gentle and respectful manner built confidence and encouraged growth. The Prophet also connected youth leadership with accountability before Allah (SWT). He once said:

> *"The feet of the son of Adam shall not move from before his Lord on the Day of Judgment until he is asked about five things..."* — among them, *"his youth and how he spent it" (Tirmidhi)*

This shows that youth is not a time to be wasted, but a divine gift entrusted to each individual.

In today's context, this Prophetic model remains deeply relevant. Mentoring young Muslims must go beyond instruction—it must involve empathy, trust, and active inclusion. Parents, teachers, and community leaders should provide spaces where youth can explore their potential, develop critical thinking, and contribute meaningfully to society.

The Quran and Sunnah both emphasise that leadership is not the domain of the aged alone. With faith, sincerity, and the right nurturing, even the youngest believers can rise to extraordinary heights. Their stories are reminders that Islam has always been a religion that values and empowers youth, not just for the future, but for the present. In every generation, the ummah must seek to identify, uplift, and support the emerging leaders among its youth, just as the Prophet did, and just as the Quran celebrates.

Chapter Six

Building Confidence and Resilience in Youth Leaders

Overcoming Self-Doubt and Building Self-Confidence

Self-doubt is one of the most common internal barriers faced by youth it quietly undermines their potential and prevents them from stepping into leadership roles. Islam offers framework that nurtures self-confidence and it is not about excessive pride or arrogance, but rather a belief in one's abilities and potential, while also recognising the importance of relying on Allah (SWT) for guidance and support.

It's about having faith in one's capacity to succeed in this life and the Hereafter while acknowledging that all power and ability ultimately come from Allah (SWT). Confidence in Muslim youth leaders must come from the understanding that they were created with divine intention and possess the capability to fulfil meaningful roles in society.

Several Quranic verses promote self-confidence and faith in Allah (SWT), emphasising the importance of depending on Him rather than oneself for support and direction. These verses emphasise the value of having faith, patience, and asking Allah (SWT) for help to overcome obstacles and develop a strong sense of self-worth.

The most frequently named prophet in the Quran is Musa (AS). The pinnacle of bravery, he is renowned for having defied the Pharaoh and stood his ground to liberate the populace from oppression. His bravery and self-assurance resulted from a very deliberate dua (supplication to Allah SWT), not of chance.

Recall that Musa (AS) was initially treated with great luxury in the Pharaoh's palace, but he had to escape and become impoverished due to a tragic catastrophe. Years later, Allah (SWT) summoned Musa (AS), still feeling guilty. On behalf of the persecuted Israelites, he must return to the Pharaoh and appeal. Musa now offers his impassioned prayer:

> *"[Moses] said, My Lord, expand for me my breast [with assurance]. And ease me my task. And untie the knot from my tongue that they may understand my speech And appoint for me a minister from my family -Aaron, my brother. Increase through him my strength that we may exalt You much, and remember You much. Indeed, You are of us ever Seeing" (Quran 20:25-35)*

In Musa's (AS) dua, Allah (SWT) demonstrates how to do it. Musa (AS) acknowledges that Allah (SWT) is the Lord and the source of all victory. He confesses his obstacle and requests its removal; in the final section, he begs for a supporter from his own family. He asks Allah (SWT) to broaden his chest and mind and ease the affair.

We hesitate even though everything around us tells us this is the best course of action. It may be giving a presentation to our coworkers, changing careers, writing an article, taking a course, or standing up for someone wronged. This feeling of overwhelm, dread, and self-doubt frequently results in unhealthy paralysis. Thankfully, we can use these emotions for our own good.

Our self-doubt or fear of failing prevents us from achieving our goals. Sometimes, we simply worry about seeming unflattering in front of others. Thus, having great confidence means that you can accomplish something and that you feel capable of doing it, or that it's okay if you don't get it exactly perfect, because that reduces the fear of failing.

The foundation of developing self-esteem is to completely rely on the Creator of the earth and the heavens and to stop depending on yourself. This is clarified for us in the Quranic verse where Allah (SWT) praises those who are patient and trust in their lord. Being patient entails being determined.

> *Allah states in the Quran, "Indeed, we have created man in the best of stature" (Quran 95:4)*

This verse is a foundational reminder of the honour bestowed upon all humans. A young Muslim leader must understand that they were created not to follow the crowd, but to lead it with vision and values. Belief in one's abilities starts with faith in one's Creator. When a young person believes that Allah (SWT) has chosen them for a specific purpose, their doubts fade.

Developing a positive mindset entails surrounding oneself with uplifting people, practising dhikr (remembrance of Allah SWT), and taking deliberate steps towards personal development.

> *The Prophet Muhammad (PBUH) taught us that optimism is a form of faith. He went on: "There is no contagion and no pessimism, but I like optimism." They asked, "What is optimism?" He said, "A good word." (Sahih Bukhari)*

According to this hadith, confidence frequently begins with positive thinking and the way we talk about ourselves and our surroundings.

In Islam, the best way to build confidence is to implement combination of spiritual practices and actions, which includes regular prayer, broaden Islamic knowledge and close relationship with Allah (SWT) and believing in Allah's (SWT) plan (Tawakkul), and doing good deeds in everyday life can help build confidence and resilience.

Self-confidence is not about perfection; it is about taking initiative with positive action. The Prophet (PBUH) encouraged his companions to take responsibility early and believed in them until they began to believe in themselves. Youth leaders today must speak up, take initiative, start taking responsibility for the community and learn from their mistakes in a positive way.

Risk-taking and learning from failures are an essential part of leadership development. Effort and sincere intention are very important factors in Islam.

> *Prophet Muhammad (PBUH) said: "All the children of Adam are sinners, and the best of sinners are those who repent." (Tirmidhi)*

This Hadith defines failure as not a result of negative thoughts, but how you respond to them.

Youth leaders must understand that setbacks are stepping stones, not dead ends. The companions of the Prophet faced failures, including at battles like Uhud, but their resilience and repentance turned those moments into growth. They learned, adapted, and continued to lead. When done with wisdom and tawakkul (trust in Allah SWT), risk-taking helps youth stretch their potential and become resilient leaders, unafraid of making mistakes in pursuit of good.

Developing Emotional Intelligence and Resilience

Emotional intelligence is the ability to understand and manage one's emotions and relate to the emotions of others. It's a critical trait for effective leadership. In day-to-day living, emotional intelligence can be useful. People with emotional intelligence are aware that while emotions might be strong, they are also fleeting. The emotionally sensible course of action would be to pause before reacting to a highly charged emotional incident, such as getting upset with a coworker. Everyone is able to control their emotions and consider all the aspects of the dispute more logically as a result.

Thinking about and empathising with other people's feelings is a big aspect of emotional intelligence. This frequently entails thinking about how you would react in a similar circumstance. Strong emotional intelligence allows one to take into account the opinions, feelings, and experiences of others and utilise this knowledge to explain why individuals act in certain ways. In addition to being skilled at imagining how others might feel, emotionally intelligent people are also skilled at comprehending their own emotions. People who are self-aware can take into account the various aspects that influence their feelings.

Self-awareness is key in bringing out the best in others since it's necessary to bring out the best in yourself first. Completing 360-degree feedback, which compares your performance to the views of your supervisor, colleagues, and direct reports, is a simple method to gauge your level of self-awareness. You will learn more about your own behaviour and how you are viewed within the company through this approach.

Leaders who struggle with self-control are more likely to react and struggle to control their impulses. Reactions are usually automatic. However, you may move from reaction to response more easily if you are more in tune with your emotional intelligence. To respond to stress and adversity more correctly and purposefully, it's critical to take a moment to gather your thoughts, breathe, and do whatever it takes to control your emotions, whether that means contacting a buddy or going for a walk. Your inner spirit keeps you going and motivates you, especially when things are tough.

Your capacity to handle interpersonal interactions, which is essential for developing empathy, productive team dynamics, and successful cooperation, can be improved with emotional intelligence. All work settings are shaped by their leaders. More serious repercussions could arise from their lack of emotional intelligence, including decreased employee engagement and a greater turnover rate.

Even if you are technically very good at your profession, your technical talents will be neglected if you cannot interact with others or communicate with your team successfully. Emotional intelligence can assist each of us in creating and preserving healthier, more robust relationships. Effective use of emotional intelligence is very beneficial for inspiring leaders.

The Quran and Hadith provide guidance on being emotionally aware and considerate, fostering positive relationships, and handling emotional situations with wisdom and patience. Youth with emotional intelligence are better able to lead with empathy, resolve conflicts, and remain grounded in difficult situations. Islam promotes emotional awareness through the regular practice of self-examination, prayer, and self-control.

One of the most emotionally intelligent figures in Islamic history was the Prophet Muhammad (PBUH). He showed empathy, patience, and awareness of the emotional states of his companions and his actions when a companion was grieving, getting angry, and confused, and then how our Prophet comforted, calmed, and corrected them peacefully.

Coping Strategies for Handling Challenges and Setbacks

Stepping into the role of a youth leader is both a blessing and a test. For Muslim youth, this responsibility goes beyond just organising events or mentoring others—it includes upholding the teachings of Islam and being a role model. While the path is rewarding, it's not free of trials. Setbacks will come in many forms: from failed plans and criticism to moments of self-doubt. These experiences don't define your ability to lead. How you face them defines you—with faith, strength, and wisdom.

One of the most powerful tools a Muslim leader has is the ability to seek comfort through their connection with Allah (SWT). When problems arise, praying and the Quran can bring clarity and peace to the heart. Remembering Allah (SWT) regularly (dhikr) helps ease anxiety and puts things into perspective. In times of stress, sincere *dua* can be a form of therapy. You are not alone in your struggles—Allah (SWT) is always listening, and your sincerity never goes unnoticed.

Patience, or sabr, is a core trait of successful leaders. Every leader will face challenges, but a Muslim youth leader can take inspiration from the Prophet Muhammad's (PBUH) life. He encountered rejection, opposition, and hardship, yet remained calm and steady in his mission. Likewise, when your efforts don't produce the expected results, or people question your decisions, responding with patience shows maturity. Pair that with tawakkul—placing your trust in Allah (SWT)—and you'll find the strength to keep going even when things get tough.

Not everything is in your control. You can put in your best effort and plan wisely, but sometimes things don't go as expected. Remember that Allah (SWT)'s wisdom surpasses ours in those moments. Accepting that some outcomes are part of a greater plan helps reduce stress. When an event doesn't go well or a group activity falls apart, treat it as a failure instead of viewing it as a lesson. There may be something valuable in the setback you don't yet understand.

Managing your emotions is also a key part of facing adversity. As a leader, your reactions influence those who look up to you. Staying composed when things go wrong sets an example of emotional control and maturity. Before reacting out of frustration or disappointment, take a step back. Ask yourself if your response reflects the kind of leader you aim to be. Avoid acting on impulse. Instead, respond thoughtfully and with kindness. This balance between emotional strength and compassion earns respect and builds trust.

No one succeeds alone. Surround yourself with supportive, like-minded individuals who understand your goals and values. Even the Prophet (PBUH) had a close group of companions who offered support and advice. As a youth leader, having a solid support system can make a big difference. Whether it's a mentor, an older community member, or a fellow youth leader, sharing your struggles and receiving feedback helps you grow. These relationships also remind you that you're not alone on this journey.

Failures, when approached with the right mindset, become stepping stones for personal growth. Maybe a plan didn't go as you wanted, or you made a mistake while handling a situation. That's okay. Every error is an opportunity to reflect and improve. Rather than criticising yourself harshly, analyse what went wrong and how you can do better next time. This self-awareness helps you become a more capable and grounded leader.

Don't ignore your well-being while serving others. Leadership can be demanding, and burnout is real. Getting enough rest, eating well, staying active, and allowing yourself time to recharge are important. Being constantly overwhelmed or exhausted makes it difficult to lead effectively. Take moments to reflect, breathe, and care for your body and mind. Islam encourages balance, and caring for yourself is part of that balance.

Revisiting your intentions helps you stay grounded. Ask yourself why you took on the role of a youth leader in the first place. If your purpose is to serve your community and seek the pleasure of Allah (SWT), don't allow temporary struggles to discourage you. Sincerity of purpose is powerful. It can keep you through the most challenging times and help you remember the greater reward with Allah (SWT).

Small wins deserve recognition. Often, leaders focus so much on long-term goals that they forget to appreciate the little things. Whether seeing someone smile because of your program or watching a shy participant gain confidence, these are signs that your efforts are making an impact. Take time to be thankful for these blessings. Practising gratitude boosts your motivation and helps shift your focus from problems to progress.

Be kind to yourself. You don't need to be perfect to be effective. Everyone makes mistakes, and part of being a good leader is learning from those mistakes. If you fall short or miss the mark, seek forgiveness, learn from the experience, and keep moving forward. A leader who is open to growth and willing to admit shortcomings becomes more approachable and relatable.

Always keep your heart connected to Allah (SWT). Make it a habit to ask for His guidance regularly, not just in moments of crisis. Pray for strength, clarity, and sincerity. A beautiful supplication to remember is: "O Allah, make difficult things easy for me, and guide me to what pleases You." With this mindset, even your toughest days can feel lighter, and you'll be reminded that success ultimately comes from Him.

In conclusion, being a Muslim youth leader is about striving, not being flawless. Challenges are part of the journey, but with faith, self-awareness, and a strong support system, you can overcome them. Remember: your impact may not always be visible immediately, but your sincerity and efforts are never wasted. Every act done for the sake of Allah (SWT) holds value, and every difficulty faced with patience brings reward. Keep leading with heart, faith, and courage.

Chapter Seven

Youth Engagement in Community Service and Activism

Importance of Community Involvement for Youth Leaders

Community involvement is not just an optional activity for young leaders—it's a responsibility and a source of personal growth. Communities' futures are greatly influenced by the participation of young people in a variety of socially good initiatives. They provide the fresh vitality, creative concepts, and viewpoints required to address today's issues. Their personal development is aided by active community participation, enabling them to embrace best practices and acquire new experiences.

When youth participate in service and activism, they step outside their comfort zones and learn how to lead with empathy, courage, and a deep understanding of people's needs. Engaging with their communities helps them see the world through different perspectives and builds the emotional intelligence and resilience that great leaders need.

Youth who participate in community activities have a sense of purpose and identity. They start to recognise their place in the community and the good impact they may have when they contribute to something bigger than themselves. Healthy self-esteem depends on having a sense of pride and belonging, which this fosters. Through community engagement, young people are also frequently exposed to various viewpoints, which deepens their awareness of the world and fosters empathy and respect for others.

Ever wondered why community is so important in Islam? Even personal acts like praying are frequently connected to group rituals. Why is it that men must offer collective prayers in the mosque? Given that the Quran instructs believers to put aside all material concerns during this holy period, why is the Friday prayer (Jummah) required?

History shows us that togetherness has always been important for growth and personal development as well as for survival. Community is a thread in the fabric of faith that binds us together in spirit and purpose. We frequently look to our community for support and direction, especially in trying times. A supportive community, whether through our family, friends, schools, jobs, or community organisations, can greatly impact our lives.

One of Islam's fundamental tenets is unity, which encompasses many different elements, including the belief in a single Lord, a single Book, a single Prophet, a single religion, a single qiblah, and a single ummah. Allah (SWT) refers to the Ummah as a single entity in all his decrees, implying that they are a single body. They are all subject to the same prohibitions and directives; there is no distinction between them.

Salah and Hajj are two of the best instances of Islam's unity and call for togetherness; everyone, regardless of wealth or lack thereof, age or ethnicity, is encouraged to go and pray in congregation. In a similar vein, everyone who can afford it is required to perform the Hajj and is expected to dress similarly. Imagine millions of people wearing the same kind of clothing in the same location at the same time. What finer symbol of solidarity could there be? No other religion requires it. In order to become strong and obstruct the path of those who plot against Islam and its people, we should all be in accord and compliance.

Islam encourages believers to keep up their interpersonal ties with other Muslims as well as their personal relationship with Allah (SWT). As a Muslim, it's your duty to participate in your community. Allah (SWT) defines the importance of community:

> *"And hold firmly to the rope of Allah all together and do not become divided..." (Quran 3:103)*

This verse serves as divine counsel on the strength of community, our relationship with the Quran, and a call for togetherness. For Muslim youth, this involvement also has a spiritual purpose. Islam teaches compassion, justice, and service to others.

> *The Prophet (PBUH) said, "The best of people are those who are most beneficial to others" (Tabarani)*

Serving the community is not only a way to grow as a leader—it's a way to live according to core Islamic principles.

By getting involved, youth also break the stereotype that young people are too inexperienced or disconnected to make a difference. Their passion, creativity, and energy often lead to fresh solutions and inspire others to take action. Leadership begins by serving, and community service is one of the most powerful ways to start that journey.

Exploring Ways to Volunteer and Community Service

Volunteer opportunities are everywhere. The key is to start with something that matches your interests and values. Whether organising a cleanup drive, tutoring younger students, helping the elderly, or working with a food bank, every small effort matters. These acts of service can create ripple effects that extend far beyond what we can see.

Local mosques, community centres, and schools often need volunteers. Youth can offer their time during weekend programs, help with event planning, or participate in outreach initiatives. Non-profit organisations also welcome young volunteers to support causes like mental health awareness, refugee aid, or environmental protection.

With technology, even virtual volunteering has become possible. From creating awareness campaigns on social media to organising online fundraisers or offering digital tutoring, there are endless ways to serve from any location. The intention matters most—to help others and grow into a responsible, giving individual.

Impact of Social Activism and Advocacy in Addressing Societal Issues

Activism and advocacy are powerful tools for change. Young people who stand up against injustice, inequality, or harmful practices become the voices that shift societal conversations. Throughout history, youth have often been at the forefront of movements that challenged the status quo and led to lasting transformation.

Social activism doesn't always mean loud protests or confrontations. It can be as simple as educating people, raising awareness through writing or speaking, or lobbying for fairer policies. Youth activists today are fighting for climate justice, better education, mental health support, and the rights of marginalised communities.

When rooted in Islamic values, advocacy becomes even more meaningful. Islam encourages speaking the truth, standing against oppression, and helping the weak. Activism becomes an act of worship when it aims to build a more just and compassionate society. It allows youth to live their values out loud, with both heart and action.

Empowering Youth to Initiate Positive Change

Young people don't need permission or resources to make a difference. Every big change starts with a small idea—and the courage to act on it. Empowerment means giving youth the tools, knowledge, and confidence to believe their voices and actions matter.

To be empowered, youth must first believe in themselves. They need to recognise that their unique skills—whether it's public speaking, organising, creative thinking, or problem-solving—can all contribute to meaningful change. Mentorship is also key. When older leaders support and guide younger ones, they create a chain of inspiration that strengthens the entire community.

Programs and workshops that teach leadership, project planning, and communication skills can help youth turn their ideas into action. But real empowerment happens when youth are trusted and given space to lead. When encouraged to start initiatives, take charge of projects, or even speak on community platforms, they feel seen, heard, and capable.

Examples of Youth-Led Initiatives and Projects Making a Difference

Across the globe, youth are leading incredible initiatives that prove age is no barrier to impact. In Pakistan, a group of teenagers created a mobile school for children in slums. In the UK, Muslim students launched a mental health campaign to support their peers struggling in silence. In Canada, young Muslims organised interfaith dialogue sessions to promote peace and understanding in their communities.

Even within smaller local communities, countless youth-led projects are creating real change. From distributing winter clothes to the homeless, to launching environmental awareness drives, to starting clubs that support refugees or disabled children, young people are showing that leadership is about doing, not just dreaming.

These examples are not exceptions. They remind us that with the right intention and effort, any youth can become a leader. It takes a heart full of compassion and a willingness to work hard for a cause bigger than oneself.

Encouraging Youth Participation in Social Causes Aligned with Islamic Values

For youth, the path of activism and service is even more rewarding when it aligns with their faith. Islam encourages kindness, justice, charity, and the protection of the environment. When youth participate in causes that reflect these values, they connect their actions to something deeper and more fulfilling.

Examples include supporting orphans and widows, raising awareness about ethical animal treatment, promoting education, fighting poverty, or standing up against racism and injustice. These are not only important social causes—they are also part of living as a responsible Muslim.

Parents, teachers, and community leaders should encourage youth to explore these areas, not just as good deeds, but as parts of their identity. Organising Quran circles that discuss community responsibility, inviting Muslim role models to speak, or creating faith-based service clubs are ways to make this connection stronger.

When young Muslims realise that activism and service are not just allowed but encouraged in Islam, they feel proud of who they are and what they stand for. It becomes easier to lead when your faith lights the way.

Chapter Eight

Leadership Skills Development for Muslim Youth

Essential Leadership Skills and Competencies for Young Muslims

Leadership is not just about holding a title—it's about making a meaningful impact, living purposefully, and inspiring others through character and action. For Muslim youth, leadership carries even more depth, rooted in values such as integrity, humility, justice, and service to humanity. Developing leadership skills helps young Muslims stand firm in their identity while becoming forces of positive change in the world.

A strong foundation in leadership begins with self-awareness. Understanding one's own strengths, weaknesses, values, and goals gives young leaders clarity and confidence. Emotional intelligence—the ability to manage one's emotions and understand others—is also vital. It fosters empathy, respect, and better decision-making, crucial in today's diverse and fast-changing society.

Muslim youth must also cultivate a strong moral compass. The life of the Prophet Muhammad (PBUH) offers timeless leadership lessons: honesty in dealings, patience under pressure, compassion for others, and unwavering commitment to justice. These aren't just religious ideals; they are essential competencies that shape effective, trustworthy leaders.

Communication and Public Speaking Skills

Humans are attracted to one another and interact with one another in many ways. Depending on the circumstances of an interaction, each person plays a variety of roles every day. Effective and transparent communication is essential in all interactions.

Have you ever been in a conversation when everything appeared to go south into conflict or confusion, no matter how hard you tried? Perhaps a straightforward request resulted in a miscommunication, or a small debate escalated into a heated dispute. We've all had this annoying experience. However, what if becoming proficient in successful communication is the secret to avoiding these pitfalls?

How you communicate greatly influences your capacity to get along with others and achieve your goals. You can handle issues and prevent conflict by having effective communication skills. A message must be correctly and clearly sent from the sender to the recipient for communication to be considered effective. Speaking or writing clearly is crucial, but so is ensuring the intended message is understood. This process requires both active listening and clear expression to achieve mutual understanding.

A leader's message can only spark change if communicated clearly and confidently. The ability to express ideas, speak with conviction, and actively listen are cornerstones of strong leadership. For Muslim youth, learning to communicate well allows them to be heard in classrooms, community spaces, workplaces, and beyond.

As leaders traverse the intricate terrain of the contemporary workplace, communication is not merely a tool; it's a fundamental component. Trust is essential to effective leadership. But without a genuine connection, this is impossible. You may genuinely learn about team members through communication, including what motivates and excites them as well as what worries, offends, or demotivates them. In turn, team members can relate to you and your vision when you communicate clearly and effectively. This is essential for establishing respect for one another, getting beyond obstacles, and eventually creating a motivated and intentional work atmosphere.

In leadership, communication is crucial because it brings teams together around a common goal. Effective leaders enthuse and encourage their colleagues by outlining their goal and the strategy to get it. Every team member feels appreciated and essential to the group's success when there is effective communication between them. It's nearly impossible to lead effectively if you are not a good communicator. The good news is that you can develop and refine abilities that will enable you to succeed in both. Here are some strategies to help you become a better communicator as a leader:

Being a leader requires you to remain composed while responding to shifting circumstances, variables, and difficulties. Adaptability in the workplace is the ability to stay flexible and react well to changing plans, duties, schedules, expectations, trends, objectives, or work procedures. Therefore, other soft skills essential to effective leadership, such as analytical, creative, interpersonal, and collaborative capabilities, are linked to adaptability.

To effectively reach and influence team members with varying communication styles, you must also be flexible in both your writing and speaking. For instance, when starting a new project, some employees could prefer a thorough written guide, while others would prefer a brief verbal instruction or synopsis. Talking to your reports early on about their communication preferences and habits will help you figure out what works best for them, even though some of this may be obvious.

Empathic leadership and communication are essential for success as a manager, director, or corporate executive. Employees will feel more appreciated and be more likely to achieve your objectives if you can better identify, acknowledge, and validate their experiences and feelings. Therefore, planning frequent communication meetings with your staff is critical to learn more about their goals, issues, and professional experiences. Being genuinely curious about the people you work with and showing personal interest in their lives is essential for developing stronger relationships and being an empathetic leader.

Effective leadership communication requires active listening. It's a skill that entails listening to others and attempting to decipher the meaning and intent of their words. Asking open-ended questions, responding to and utilising non-verbal clues, staying focused on the conversation, refraining from interruptions, passing judgement or offering advice, and thinking back on what you've heard are all basic active listening strategies. Understanding and empathising should be the main objectives of active listening, not reacting.

Leaders who engage in active listening can build deeper relationships with their teams by demonstrating that their thoughts and opinions are respected and heard. You may foster fruitful dialogue, establish trust, and provide an opportunity to better understand your employees' motivations, difficulties, and objectives when you know when to talk and when to listen. Keeping your body language open is a crucial part of active communication. This entails listening with a smile and a nod, maintaining eye contact, and not folding your arms.

Employees can be empowered to take calculated risks, freely express their opinions, work together more effectively and creatively, and actively solve problems by fostering an environment of openness and trust. Whether the information is positive or negative, being transparent means being upfront and honest with your team about your business's high-level objectives, difficulties, and possibilities. Transparency is essential for performance because it will inform your staff and foster confidence within your team.

By setting up clear lines of communication, clearly defining expectations, and giving regular updates on how your team and company are achieving their objectives, you may contribute to developing a transparent workplace culture. Establishing an open atmosphere where staff members feel free to voice their ideas when they disagree with management is also essential. This may entail conducting anonymous surveys regularly or setting up brief meetings to check in and give staff members a chance to ask questions or express their opinions.

When there is a lack of trust or openness in the workplace, employee stress rises, communication and morale degrade, and productivity falls. However, you can establish an environment where your team feels comfortable exploring—and expressing—their creativity if you are open, honest, and vulnerable with them, and you are willing to share discoveries and discuss justifications. Employees who participate in decision-making are more likely to feel engaged and devoted to your company, which is advantageous for all parties.

If you assume a leadership position, it will be your duty to provide constructive criticism and take it seriously. Regular communication that offers constructive criticism allows your staff members to make necessary corrections, capitalise on their strengths, and increase their general efficacy and efficiency. Focusing on the behaviour rather than the person, alternating between positive and negative remarks, and using concrete examples to back up your claims rather than generalisations are some strategies to help you give constructive criticism.

Receiving input from your staff is equally crucial if you want to improve as a leader. Effective leaders understand that they are not perfect and need to keep learning and improving. And those who are most impacted by your leadership abilities are the best people to offer helpful critiques. When receiving feedback from team members, it's critical to be open and conscious of your tone of voice and body language. You should also attempt to be impartial rather than defensive, ask clarifying questions when necessary, and evaluate the input to develop a suitable action plan.

In summary, effective communication is the foundation of strong leadership, fostering trust, collaboration, and adaptability within a team. By listening actively, being transparent, and offering constructive feedback, leaders can inspire and empower those they lead. Mastering communication skills is not just helpful—it's essential for achieving goals, building relationships, and driving meaningful change.

In a similar way, public speaking is also a crucial part of effective leadership, while intimidating for many, and it can be mastered with practice. Whether it's leading a school assembly, addressing a community gathering, or speaking at a youth forum, each experience builds confidence. Clarity of thought, proper tone, body language, and the ability to connect with an audience are all skills that grow with each effort.

Active listening is just as important. A good leader doesn't just speak—they listen deeply, understand concerns, and respectfully respond. This builds trust and ensures that everyone feels valued. Communication is a two-way street, and those who master both speaking and listening become powerful influencers.

For young Muslims, having a strong voice is also a way to represent their faith with pride. In a world full of misunderstandings, speaking about one's values with wisdom and respect can break barriers and build bridges.

Teamwork and Collaboration in Leadership Roles

No leader succeeds alone. Behind every successful mission is a team working together toward a shared vision. Learning how to collaborate, delegate, and motivate others is vital to becoming an effective leader. For youth, this means learning to lead with people, not over them.

Teamwork begins with mutual respect. Every person brings unique skills and perspectives. A wise leader recognises this and makes space for everyone's voice. In group settings, Muslim youth should strive to encourage participation, resolve conflicts peacefully, and ensure that no one is left behind.

Working as part of a team also means learning humility. Sometimes leadership means stepping back and letting others shine. Other times, it means lifting someone else's idea and helping it grow. True leaders care more about the mission than their ego.

In Islamic tradition, the concept of shura (mutual consultation) emphasises group decision-making and valuing input from all members. Youth who practise teamwork in this way not only build strong groups—they strengthen the bonds of unity and trust within their communities.

Strategic Thinking and Decision-Making

Any leader needs to be able to think strategically. It entails having the capacity to assess opportunities and challenges and come to wise decisions that advance your overarching objectives. It also entails planning, developing, and anticipating the future. Leaders may remain ahead of the competition and make wise judgments by using strategic thinking. In simple words, strategic thinking is the capacity to assess opportunities and challenges and make wise choices that advance your overarching objectives.

Every leader faces moments when tough choices must be made. Developing the ability to think ahead, weigh options, and act wisely under pressure is essential. Strategic thinking allows youth to set long-term goals, identify resources, and navigate challenges with clarity and purpose.

Planning is a key part of strategy, whether organising an event or leading a campaign, success starts with a clear roadmap. Young leaders must learn to anticipate outcomes, prepare for setbacks, and stay adaptable when circumstances change.

Strategic planning allows leaders to establish goals and objectives, recognise possible risks and opportunities, and create plans of action to achieve those goals. Additionally, it enables leaders to stay ahead of the competition by fostering an innovative and collaborative organisational culture. Leaders who comprehend the value of strategic planning will be better able to make choices that will ultimately benefit their company.

While operational planning helps manage short-term goals, strategic planning assists leaders in developing long-term plans for success. Effective leadership requires both forms of planning. After developing a strategy, it's critical to evaluate its efficacy.

This entails assessing how successfully the strategy has achieved the predetermined objectives and determining whether the plan needs revision or adjustment. Gathering data and information regarding the outcomes of plan implementation is part of the process of evaluating a strategy. You can guarantee your company's long-term success by routinely reviewing your plan and making the required modifications.

Leaders and their teams can benefit much from strategic planning. A well-written strategic plan may give the company a clear path forward and make sure that everyone is working towards the same goals. It can also assist leaders in improved decision-making and work prioritisation. Leaders may lower risks and increase their chances of success by taking the time to plan.

Efficient utilisation of resources is another benefit of strategic planning. Leaders might evaluate their budget and available resources to decide what investments are necessary to achieve their objectives. They can prevent costly errors and waste resources on pointless operations by having a plan in place. Leaders can also foster an atmosphere of accountability with the aid of strategic planning. Lastly, strategic planning can provide leaders with a feeling of command over their company. Leaders can be sure they are taking the appropriate actions to advance their team by having a strategy in place.

Decision-making also requires courage. Sometimes, the right choice isn't the easiest one. Sometimes, it involves taking a stand, saying no, or facing criticism. Muslim youth should be guided by their faith and conscience in such moments. Trust in Allah (SWT) and commitment to what's right are the pillars of strong, ethical leadership.

Learning from mistakes is also part of strategic growth. Each wrong turn is a lesson that builds resilience and insight. The more youth engage in decisions and reflect on the results, the more confident and capable they become as leaders.

Problem-Solving Techniques and Critical Thinking Abilities

Leaders are often looked to for answers, especially in difficult situations. That's why problem-solving and critical thinking are such vital tools. They help youth break down challenges, analyse situations fairly, and come up with innovative, effective solutions.

Problem-solving begins with curiosity, asking questions like "Why is this happening?" or "What are the root causes?" leads to deeper understanding. From there, exploring various solutions, testing ideas, and choosing the best path forward becomes much easier.

Critical thinking is about seeing beyond surface-level information. It helps youth examine situations from all angles, separate emotion from logic, and avoid jumping to conclusions. It also means being open to new ideas and willing to change one's mind when presented with better evidence.

For Muslim youth, the Quran and teachings of the Prophet encourage reflection, seeking knowledge, and thoughtful decision-making. These values align perfectly with modern critical thinking. By combining faith with intellect, youth can solve problems in wise and compassionate ways.

Real-world leadership often demands thinking on your feet. Whether it's managing a group crisis, resolving conflict, or addressing an unexpected challenge, young leaders with sharp problem-solving skills can lead their teams through anything with grace and focus.

Balancing Creativity with Responsibility in Leadership

Great leaders are not only strategic—they are also creative. They think outside the box, take bold steps, and find new ways to inspire others. But creativity in leadership must always be paired with responsibility. Ideas may be exciting but must also be grounded, realistic, and ethical.

Creativity allows youth to bring fresh energy to old challenges. It could mean introducing new methods for community outreach, finding unique ways to engage peers, or developing innovative campaigns that get people excited. Imaginative leaders stand out and spark inspiration in others.

But leadership also carries responsibility. Creative leaders must consider the consequences of their actions, stay true to their values, and ensure that their innovations serve the greater good. In Islamic teachings, every person is accountable for their actions. This means being mindful of how leadership choices affect others.

Young leaders must learn to balance passion with purpose. An exciting idea must also be inclusive, practical, and beneficial. This balance ensures that creativity is not just fun—but meaningful.

Accountability also means following through. It's easy to come up with ideas, but real leadership means seeing them through to the end, even when challenges arise. It's about doing the hard work behind the scenes and owning both the successes and the setbacks.

Leadership is a journey—a path of growth, service, and self-discovery. For Muslim youth, it's a journey enriched by the values of Islam, the wisdom of tradition, and the vibrant potential of the future. Developing leadership skills isn't just about becoming someone others follow; it's about becoming someone others trust, admire, and learn from.

Every young Muslim has the ability to lead—with the right mindset, tools, and faith. The world is full of challenges, but also full of opportunities. Step up. Lead with heart. Think boldly. Act justly. And remember that the best leaders are those who lead by example, guided by the light of truth and the strength of faith.

Chapter Nine

Ethical Leadership and Islamic Values

Importance of Ethics and Integrity in Youth Leadership

Leadership without ethics is like a compass without a needle. It might carry power, but it lacks direction. For Muslim youth stepping into leadership roles—whether in schools, communities, or larger platforms—ethics and integrity must serve as the foundation of their actions. When young leaders prioritise moral character over popularity or personal gain, they create an environment of trust, respect, and long-lasting impact.

Ethics in leadership means doing the right thing, even when it's hard or unpopular. It's about staying true to one's values in every decision and interaction. For Muslim youth, ethical leadership is not only about good character—it's a reflection of faith in action. Leading with integrity shows a commitment to truthfulness, fairness, and responsibility, all of which are deeply embedded in Islamic teachings.

When a leader is honest and upright, people naturally follow. Integrity builds credibility, and credibility inspires others. This kind of leadership doesn't just influence projects or programs—it shapes hearts and minds. In a world where ethical lapses are common in leadership at every level, young Muslim leader who walk with honesty and humility can truly stand out and lead a new era of trust-based leadership.

Upholding Islamic Principles of Honesty, Fairness, and Accountability

Islamic teachings emphasise the importance of living an honest, fair, and accountable life. The Quran and Sunnah repeatedly stress values that are not only spiritual obligations but also practical principles for ethical leadership. For youth stepping into leadership roles, embodying honesty, fairness, and accountability is not just ideal—it's essential for success and lasting influence. The foundation of trust is integrity and dependability. Without these attributes, trust is lost, and leadership fails.

By his example, the Holy Prophet Muhammad (PBUH) demonstrated that he was the most honest and truthful person of his time. He was a penniless orphan who began trading with his uncle, but he quickly gained fame and respect because of his fair and honest dealings with everyone. He was known to all Meccans, regardless of wealth, as Al-Amin (the Trustworthy) and As-Sadiq (the Truthful).

Near Mount Safa, the Prophet once assembled the whole Quraysh population and commanded them, "O Quraysh! Will you believe me if I tell you an army is moving towards you from behind the mountains? "Yes, because we have never heard you tell a lie," they all responded.

Every single person in Mecca vowed to be honest and truthful because he had spent forty years living a pure and deeply religious life among them. However, the majority of them continued to reject him as Allah's Messenger. Even his most ardent adversaries admitted that he had lived his entire life among them in virtue and purity. They knew that he was the most sincere and honest of them all.

For his disciples and for all believers throughout history, the Prophet (PBUH) established an example. He is, in fact, the example that Allah (SWT) has given us. Therefore, any authentic Muslim leader is aware that Allah (SWT) is the source of all power and success, even if he shows total dedication to his position and duty.

Being trustworthy allows a person to not only fulfil Allah's (SWT) order but also exhibit positive attitudes that are universally recognised and carry out assigned responsibilities and duties transparently, improving perception and fostering trust. Overall, it can be claimed that the foundation of leadership is reliability.

The ability of a leader to perform their duties in accordance with Allah's (SWT) instructions in the Quran determines their level of success. A leader should be trustworthy since everyone has a moral obligation to trust others when doing their duties. When a leader controls and administers their leadership because of Allah (SWT), they are performing a sunnah. If a leader can guide their people to the path Allah (SWT) wills, they will be rewarded with paradise.

This trait was demonstrated by the Prophet Muhammad (PBUH) even before he became a prophet. The inhabitants of Mecca famously referred to him as Al-Amin, meaning the Trustworthy. Various tribes disputed where to put the sacred Black Stone during the reconstruction of the Kaaba, but they decided to let the next person enter to make the decision.

Because they trusted Prophet Muhammad (PBUH) to be honest and fair, everyone accepted his decision without question. This instance demonstrates how integrity enhances authority and reputation. Being sincere in their endeavours, transparent in their communication, and truthful in their objectives not only garners respect but also lays the groundwork for solid, long-lasting leadership for today's youth.

Fairness, or adl, is another essential trait. An ethical leader does not play favourites or allow personal feelings to affect decisions.

The Quran commands, "Indeed, Allah commands you to render trusts to whom they are due and when you judge between people to judge with justice" (Quran 4:58)

A beautiful example from Islamic history is the leadership of Caliph Umar ibn al-Khattab (RA).

Umar bin Khattab (RA), whose full name is Umar bin Khattab bin Nufail, is a descendant of Abdul Uzza Al-Quraisy and a member of the aristocratic Adi tribe. As-Sabiqunal Awwalun, or the early Muslims, is a group of which Umar bin Khattab (RA) is a member. Before the hijrah, he professed his religion before the Prophet (PBUH) in Mecca. He also stayed with the Prophet (PBUH) during all of the major events and wars in Medina. Before his eventual conversion to Islam, Umar (RA) was a vicious individual who harboured deep hatred for the Prophet Muhammad (PBUH).

When Caliph Umar bin Khattab (RA) learnt that his sister, Fatimah bint Al-Khattab, and her husband, Said bin Zaid, had converted to Islam, he was first incensed but was soon persuaded to follow suit. He felt a deep longing to meet the Messenger of Allah (PBUH), and his heart melted. At last, he bowed down before the Prophet (PBUH) and professed his faith in Islam. Umar bin Khattab (RA) was sworn in as the second caliph following the death of Abu Bakr (RA) Ash-Shiddiq. He was regarded as an exceptional leader who consistently paid attention to the needs of the average person and upheld justice.

Umar bin Khattab's name has been cited more than any other person in Islamic history, aside from the Messenger of Allah (PBUH). The name is pronounced with reverence and awe when connected to everything known about him, such as his magnificence and genius. While talking about zuhud (renunciation of worldly pleasures), one is reminded of Umar's (RA).

When someone mentions perfect and flawless justice, Umar's (RA) justice immediately springs to mind. When someone talks about honesty, whether or not they are near relatives, they are reminded of Umar's (RA) honesty; the same is true when someone talks about profound knowledge and Islamic law.

Caliph Umar bin Khattab (RA) was not content with his position despite being a powerful leader at the time. Umar (RA) continued to have a modest life. He had no qualms about sharing his property with those in need or offering it to Allah (SWT). Both Umar's (RA) way of living and his attire demonstrated his simplicity. After capturing Jerusalem, he entered there in tattered clothing and displayed a great deal of humility.

Social justice was one of the main characteristics of 'Umar ibn al Khattab (RA) that best represented his personality. According to him, social justice entails redistributing wealth and power so that, when implemented at the lowest level, it eventually spreads to all societal levels. He created the foundations of justice, Al Adl, throughout history. 'Umar (RA) established the first social policy infrastructure.

He created the idea of Bait ul Maal (RA). At night, he would wander the streets of Medina to assist his people. He laid the groundwork for the modern West's adoption of child benefit or children's allowance, which provides weekly payments to all children to help them survive.

Umar (RA) had a reputation for being fair. When his son was once charged with a crime, Umar (RA) did not excuse him; instead, he held him to the same level as everyone else. In another tale, a Muslim commander was the target of a complaint from a non-Muslim civilian. After personally looking at the complaint, Umar (RA) decided in favour of the non-Muslim and deemed it to be legitimate.

These instances tell us that justice must cut across racial, religious, and social boundaries. Everywhere they lead young leaders who respect justice, foster an environment of equality and trust. Umar bin Khattab (RA) is one of the many significant Islamic figures who exemplify leadership values. The current generation might look up to the example set by Caliph Umar bin Khattab (RA).

Accountability is the third cornerstone of ethical leadership. Islam teaches that each soul is responsible for their deeds.

> *"Every one of you is a shepherd and every one of you is responsible for his flock" (Sahih Bukhari)*

Leadership is a responsibility, not a privilege. Umar ibn al-Khattab (RA) again provides a strong example.

He once said, "If a mule stumbles in Iraq, I fear that Allah (SWT) will ask me why I did not level the road for it." Such deep accountability reflects how seriously a leader should take their duties. Umar (RA) did not shift blame; he considered himself answerable even for minor issues under his rule.

When modern young leaders hold themselves accountable, they foster a team culture that values honesty, responsibility, and growth. Instead of hiding mistakes or blaming others, they accept shortcomings, seek feedback, and work towards improvement. This humility strengthens their credibility and inspires others to act responsibly, too.

In sum, Islamic teachings guide leaders to be honest, fair, and accountable. The examples of Prophet Muhammad (PBUH) and his rightly guided successors show how these values are not abstract ideals but living principles. For youth preparing to take on leadership roles, practising these values is not merely beneficial; it's a duty.

Leadership in Islam is seen as an amanah (trust), and fulfilling this trust with honesty, fairness, and accountability ensures success in this world and reward in the hereafter. By reflecting on these examples from Islamic history and striving to embody these qualities, young leaders can truly make a positive and lasting difference in their communities.

Addressing Ethical Dilemmas Faced by Young Leaders

Leadership is not always black and white. Often, youth in leadership roles face tough ethical dilemmas that test their values. Whether it's peer pressure, competing interests, or the temptation to take shortcuts, such challenges demand courage and clarity of principle.

One common dilemma is choosing between popularity and integrity. It's easy to go along with the crowd or make decisions that win favour, but ethical leadership means choosing what is right over what is easy. For instance, a young leader might face pressure to overlook misconduct in a team to avoid conflict. Yet, Islam teaches us to stand for truth, even when it's uncomfortable.

Another frequent challenge is handling power and influence. Some may feel tempted to misuse their position for personal benefit or recognition. The Prophet Muhammad (PBUH) warned against seeking leadership for selfish reasons and reminded us that leadership is a responsibility and a trust (amanah), not a prize to be claimed.

Financial temptations, peer influence, and fear of criticism can also test a young leader's ethical resolve. The best way to handle such moments is to turn back to Islamic values, seek counsel from wise mentors, and pray for strength. Islam provides a moral compass that helps youth navigate uncertainty with confidence and clarity.

Applying Islamic Values in Leadership Practices

Ethical leadership goes far beyond simply staying away from wrongdoing. True leadership means actively living out good values in everyday actions and decisions. For Muslim youth, especially, leadership should be shaped and guided by the teachings of Islam, influencing how they speak, act, decide, and serve others.

One key value a young Muslim leader must carry is humility (tawadu'). Humility is not just about being modest; it's about truly seeing oneself as equal to others, no matter one's achievements or position. The Prophet Muhammad (PBUH) set the ultimate example of humility. Even though he was the greatest leader in history, he lived simply.

He would sit with the poor, serve his neighbours, and treat everyone respectfully, never acting superior. Muslim youth who take on leadership roles can mirror this by making it a habit to listen more than they speak, acknowledge the contributions of others, and put the needs of the group ahead of personal pride. Leadership is not about being above others; it's about lifting others up.

Another essential value is sincerity (Ikhlas). Sincerity means doing things for the right reasons — seeking Allah's (SWT) pleasure rather than fame, approval, or personal gain. A young leader must regularly check their intentions. Are they stepping up to lead a project to genuinely help their community, or are they looking for recognition?

Whether organising a school event, managing a community fundraiser, or leading a student group, the heart behind the action matters most. Sincere leadership leads to real, lasting impact, while leadership driven by ego tends to crumble under pressure. Young leaders must constantly renew their intentions and remind themselves that true success comes from earning Allah's (SWT) approval, not applause from people.

Leadership involves making decisions that affect others' lives, and every word or action taken can have ripple effects. Muslim youth should view leadership opportunities as amanah given by Allah (SWT) to be protected and honoured. Slacking off, making careless decisions, or breaking promises is a betrayal of that trust. Instead, they should strive to fulfil their responsibilities to the best of their abilities, knowing Allah (SWT) watches over every effort.

Ethical leadership for Muslim youth is not about perfection; it's about consistently aligning one's actions with Islamic values. Mistakes will happen, but what matters is the willingness to correct them, seek forgiveness, and continue improving. Young leaders should also surround themselves with good advisors and friends who will remind them to stay humble, sincere, and trustworthy.

Ultimately, leadership is a form of service. It's about helping others, improving communities, and standing up for what is right. By building their leadership on humility, sincerity, and trust, Muslim youth can make a real difference in the world around them. They not only inspire others through their actions but also earn blessings in this life and the next. When leadership becomes an act of worship and a reflection of faith, it transforms both the leader and those they serve. In a world that often rewards arrogance and selfish ambition, leading with Islamic values becomes a powerful and beautiful act of resistance and hope.

Promoting Justice, Compassion, and Inclusivity in Leadership Roles

True Islamic leadership is a force that lifts others. It is grounded in the principles of justice, fueled by compassion, and dedicated to welcoming every voice. When Muslim youth leaders live by these values, they create spaces that are not only safe but deeply empowering for all those they serve. Their leadership becomes a light that guides others towards fairness, kindness, and community.

Justice in Islamic leadership is far more than simply being fair. It is about actively standing against oppression and making sure that every individual is treated with dignity and respect. Whether it's confronting bullying at school, speaking up against racism, or challenging unfair treatment in society, a true leader cannot stay silent.

The Quran instructs believers to be "bearers of witness with justice," even if it means standing against themselves or their own families. This highlights how central justice is to leadership—it demands courage, honesty, and a deep sense of responsibility. Muslim youth leaders who commit to justice understand that their role is not just to lead, but to advocate for what is right, even when difficult.

Alongside justice, compassion—known in Arabic as rahmah—is a foundation of ethical leadership. The Prophet Muhammad (PBUH) led with immense love, patience, and care, especially for society's most vulnerable members. His leadership was never harsh or dismissive; instead, it reflected deep empathy and understanding.

Today's young Muslim leaders must carry forward this legacy of compassion. They should be approachable, gentle, and patient with those they serve. Compassionate leadership builds bridges instead of walls. It creates communities where individuals feel supported and uplifted rather than judged or excluded. When leaders approach others with genuine care, they nurture environments where everyone can grow and thrive.

Inclusivity is another vital pillar of true Islamic leadership. Every group, organisation, or community brings together a variety of talents, perspectives, and backgrounds. A good leader recognises the beauty and strength in this diversity. Ethical leadership ensures that every person is respected, valued, and given a chance to contribute.

No one should feel sidelined because of their abilities, cultural background, gender, or personal beliefs. Instead, a leader must create spaces where everyone feels seen, heard, and motivated to participate. Inclusivity is not just about being open-minded; it's about actively working to make sure that every person knows they are an important part of the community.

By practising justice, compassion, and inclusivity, Muslim youth leaders can transform the environments they lead. They inspire trust, foster collaboration, and help build communities that reflect the true spirit of Islam. Their leadership becomes an example to others, showing that real strength lies in serving with integrity, kindness, and fairness. Such leadership not only helps individuals feel safe and empowered but also contributes to a more just and caring society.

In the end, Islamic leadership is not about holding power over others. It's about serving with humility and lifting others. It calls for a deep commitment to the values taught by the Prophet Muhammad (PBUH) and emphasised in the Quran. Muslim youth today have a powerful opportunity to lead with these timeless principles—standing firmly for justice, breathing life into communities with compassion, and embracing all voices with open hearts. When they do so, they honour the true essence of leadership in Islam and inspire others to do the same.

Establishing Ethical Guidelines Based on Quranic Teachings and Prophetic Examples

To ensure ethical leadership is not left to chance or interpretation, young leaders must establish clear guidelines rooted in Islam. These principles become the moral code that guides decisions, actions, and the overall direction of leadership.

Start by grounding leadership in the Quran. Verses that emphasise justice, truthfulness, mercy, and responsibility can be turned into action steps. For example, Surah Al-Ma'idah teaches:

> *"Do not let the hatred of a people prevent you from being just. Be just: that is nearer to piety." (Quran 5:8)*

This principle reminds leaders to uphold fairness, even when emotions run high.

Prophetic leadership is also rich with examples. The Prophet (PBUH) always consulted others before making decisions, encouraged forgiveness over revenge, and led with empathy. His life serves as a living manual of ethical leadership that Muslim youth can emulate in every aspect of their role.

Creating a simple set of personal leadership ethics can also help. This might include a pledge to always tell the truth, to seek advice before making big decisions, to take accountability for mistakes, and to treat every team member with respect. Such a code keeps leaders anchored in values, especially during moments of challenge. Ethical leadership is not an option—it's a necessity. For Muslim youth, it's also an opportunity to rise above the noise and lead with light. When leadership is rooted in faith, guided by integrity, and powered by compassion, it becomes transformative.

The world is waiting for leaders who not only talk about values but live them—leaders who serve, uplift, and unite, leaders who lead not just with words but with example. If you're a young Muslim stepping into leadership, know that your ethics are your greatest strength. Stand tall, stay grounded in your values, and lead with purpose. The legacy you build will not just influence your peers—it will echo for generations to come.

Chapter Ten

Mentorship and Role Modelling for Youth Leaders

Role of Mentors and Role Models in Youth Development

Every young person has potential waiting to be unlocked. While natural talent and ambition play important roles, guidance often makes the difference between potential that fades or that which flourishes. Mentors and role models are the catalysts that turn dreams into direction.

Mentors are individuals who walk beside young people, offering wisdom, advice, and encouragement. Role models, on the other hand, inspire through action and example. Both are crucial in shaping the journey of a youth leader. They light the path, help navigate challenges, and provide a living example of what successful, values-driven leadership looks like.

In Islam, the concept of mentorship is deeply embedded. The Prophet Muhammad (PBUH) mentored his companions with love, wisdom, and patience. His mentorship gave rise to some of the greatest leaders the world has ever seen—like Abu Bakr (RA), Umar ibn al-Khattab (RA), and Ali ibn Abi Talib (RA)—all of whom learned under his care. The mentorship model he embodied wasn't just about teaching; it was about nurturing character and building confidence.

Young Muslim leaders today, just like the companions then, benefit immensely from having someone they can turn to. Someone who listens without judgment, guides with sincerity, and pushes them to grow without fear. A good mentor helps youth stay connected to their values and see their own potential, no matter the pressures they face.

Benefits of Mentorship for Aspiring Leaders

We must discover how to accomplish more tasks more quickly while using less. We must take responsibility for our professional development in this new workplace while also advancing our company. Mentoring is an effective technique that is frequently underutilised.

It offers a methodical but adaptable approach to learning in which seasoned leaders impart their wisdom to less seasoned peers while also learning from their mentees. This partnership fosters a culture of cooperation and support among leaders and speeds up their development. Mentoring helps people handle complexity, develop resilience, and adjust to change in today's fast-paced corporate environment—skills that are essential for effective leadership.

The learning curve in leadership can be steep, but mentorship helps speed up the process. Without guidance, young leaders may spend years learning lessons the hard way. A mentor shortens that timeline by sharing valuable experiences—stories of both success and failure that offer important insights. Learning from these experiences helps mentees avoid common mistakes and adopt effective strategies early, giving them a head start on their leadership path.

Mentorship also opens doors to new opportunities. Connections often play a key role in advancing careers, and mentors usually have access to established networks. They can introduce mentees to influential figures, recommend them for leadership roles, or simply create chances to gain real-world experience. These opportunities not only build a young leader's resume but also help them demonstrate their abilities on bigger platforms.

Emotional support from a mentor can be just as important as practical advice. Leadership can sometimes feel isolating, and self-doubt can be a heavy burden. Knowing someone believes in you even during your lowest moments can fuel resilience. A mentor acts as a consistent source of encouragement, celebrating milestones and inspiring their mentee to push forward even when challenges arise.

Soft skills are another critical area where mentorship makes a lasting impact. Communication, emotional intelligence, conflict resolution, and adaptability are vital traits for effective leadership. Through regular interaction, mentees learn by observing how their mentor navigates complex interpersonal situations. They pick up the nuances of empathy, active listening, and thoughtful dialogue—skills that textbooks rarely teach but are essential for building strong, cohesive teams.

Mentorship also fosters a growth mindset. By hearing their mentor's stories of setbacks and how they overcame them, young leaders begin to view failure not as defeat but as an opportunity for growth. They become more resilient and persistent, better prepared to face the inevitable challenges of leadership.

Accountability is another often-overlooked benefit. A mentor encourages goal-setting and follows up to ensure progress, helping mentees develop habits of discipline, focus, and responsibility. Over time, this accountability strengthens their leadership style, influencing how they lead others and manage projects.

Mentorship nurtures a deeper sense of purpose. Rather than chasing titles or external validation, young leaders are encouraged to connect with what truly drives them. Purposeful leadership is not only more ethical but also more sustainable over the long term.

Ultimately, mentorship often evolves into a lifelong relationship, offering support, wisdom, and encouragement across different stages of a leader's journey. For anyone aspiring to lead with impact, finding a mentor can be one of the most powerful steps they take.

Finding Suitable Mentors within the Muslim Community

In the Muslim community, mentors come from many walks of life. They may be teachers, community leaders, professionals, imams, or elder family members, each offering valuable lessons through their experiences. True mentors are not defined solely by their success, but by the way they live according to Islamic values. Their actions and character often speak louder than their achievements, guiding young people toward leadership with integrity and faith.

When seeking a mentor, young Muslims should look beyond professional success and focus on personal qualities. A good mentor listens with patience, encourages open dialogue, and builds trust. Their lifestyle should reflect Islamic teachings—demonstrating kindness, fairness, humility, and justice. Their character, more than their advice, leaves a lasting impact.

Youth must actively seek mentors rather than waiting for them to appear. Attending Islamic lectures, conferences, and volunteering at community events can create opportunities for mentorship. Approaching respected individuals with sincerity and readiness to learn opens doors to meaningful relationships. Sometimes, when mentors are not readily available nearby, young people can turn to books, lectures, podcasts, and online platforms where Muslim scholars, entrepreneurs, and leaders share their wisdom.

Learning from the rich history of Islam also offers timeless mentorship. The lives of the Prophet Muhammad (PBUH), his companions, and figures like Umar ibn al-Khattab and Salahuddin Ayyubi provide powerful examples of ethical leadership rooted in faith.

Ultimately, mentorship in Islam is about nurturing the whole person—strengthening faith, building character, and developing responsibility toward the community and beyond. With patience, prayer, and sincere effort, young Muslims can find mentors who will help them grow into leaders of purpose and integrity, whether through personal interaction or learning from a distance.

Responsibilities of Youth Leaders as Role Models

While young people need mentors to guide them, they must also recognise an important truth: the moment they step into leadership, they themselves become role models. Leadership is not just about making decisions or leading projects—it's about setting an example that others, especially those younger or less experienced, will observe and often imitate. Whether they realise it or not, someone is always watching. It might be a younger sibling, a classmate, a teammate, or a fellow volunteer. Through their actions, words, and attitudes, youth leaders have the power to shape the behaviour and values of others.

Being a role model is a serious responsibility, not a title or a badge of honour. It requires acting with integrity even when no one is watching, making decisions based on principle rather than seeking popularity, and uplifting others with kindness and fairness. True role models understand that leadership is not about being perfect—it's about being real, responsible, and reliable. They accept their flaws with humility, learn from their mistakes, and continue striving to do better, inspiring those around them through their commitment and sincerity.

In Islam, leadership is not something to be sought for personal pride or gain. It is an amanah—a sacred trust that must be honoured with honesty, justice, and service.

If a youth leader speaks respectfully, others will notice and begin to value respectful communication. If a leader stands firmly for fairness and justice, others will feel empowered to do the same. If a leader takes responsibility for their actions and does not shift blame when mistakes occur, they will inspire a culture of accountability among their peers. Leadership by example is the most powerful and enduring form of leadership. It teaches without needing to lecture. It uplifts without needing to command. It creates a ripple effect where positive actions and values naturally spread from one person to another.

To live up to this responsibility, youth leaders must constantly reflect on their intentions and actions. They must ask themselves, "Am I acting in a way that honours my faith and my trust as a leader? Am I setting an example that others would benefit from following?" This level of self-awareness is critical. Leadership is not about being perfect; it's about striving toward excellence and sincerity in every interaction.

Moreover, part of being a responsible role model is showing others how to navigate challenges and setbacks. Life will inevitably bring failures, disappointments, and moments of weakness. A true role model does not hide these experiences or pretend to be invincible. Instead, they demonstrate resilience, patience, and trust in Allah (SWT) during difficult times. They show that strength is in never falling, but in getting back up with faith, humility, and renewed determination. This realness makes them relatable and trustworthy, qualities that young followers deeply respect and admire.

Youth leaders must also cultivate a spirit of service. Leadership is not about seeking status or recognition; it's about serving others sincerely for the sake of Allah (SWT). Acts of service, no matter how small, carry immense weight. Whether it's helping organise an event, mentoring a younger student, cleaning up after a gathering, or simply offering a kind word to someone struggling—each act reflects the leader's character and influences those around them to do the same.

Building a supportive and ethical community starts with individuals who embody the values they wish to see. If young leaders are honest, generous, respectful, and committed to justice, they will inspire their communities to move in the same direction. If they are careless, selfish, or dismissive of others, they risk setting negative patterns that will be much harder to break. Every action matters. Every interaction is an opportunity to set an example that uplifts others.

The responsibility of being a role model may feel heavy at times, but it's also an incredible honour. Through their sincerity and dedication, youth leaders have the opportunity to make lasting impacts—not only on individuals but on entire communities. Their influence will stretch far beyond what they see today, shaping the attitudes, dreams, and character of future generations.

Ultimately, the greatest leadership is that which mirrors the leadership of the Prophet Muhammad (PBUH)—leadership rooted in mercy, justice, compassion, and unwavering commitment to truth. Youth leaders who embrace their role with humility, sincerity, and a desire to please Allah (SWT) will find that their efforts are blessed and their impact enduring.

As we nurture our young leaders today, let us remind and say to them: You are not just leading a project or a group. You are shaping hearts. You are lighting the way for others. And by doing so, you are fulfilling a noble trust that carries rewards not just in this life, but in the Hereafter as well.

Impact of Positive Role Modelling on Youth Behaviour and Aspirations

Positive role modelling plays a crucial role in shaping the behaviour, values, and dreams of young people. When youth see someone they admire acting with confidence, integrity, and compassion, it leaves a powerful and lasting impression on their hearts and minds. A positive role model becomes a mirror, showing young people not just who they are, but who they can become. They expand the vision of possibility, helping youth imagine greater futures for themselves that align with their deepest values.

This influence is especially strong during the teenage years, a period when identity is being shaped and personal values are being formed. Adolescents search for examples to follow, and they often look to the people around them to understand how to live with purpose and confidence. For Muslim youth, having role models who uphold Islamic principles while thriving in their communities is incredibly important. When they see leaders who pray on time, who are honest in their dealings, who treat others with kindness, and who stand bravely for justice, it sends a powerful message. It shows that faith and success are not opposing forces but can walk hand-in-hand. It tells them, "You can reach high goals without compromising your faith. You can earn respect without giving up your values."

The impact of these living examples cannot be overstated. Youth are more likely to imitate actions than to obey instructions. A thousand speeches about kindness may not have the same effect as one act of kindness witnessed at the right moment. When a young person watches a respected leader humbly serve food at a community event or stay behind to clean up after a gathering, it leaves a stronger message than any lecture about humility and service. These everyday actions plant seeds in the hearts of youth, seeds that grow into values like responsibility, compassion, and integrity.

The ripple effect of positive role-modelling is profound. One good role model can inspire not just one youth but many. When a young person is deeply moved by a leader's example, they often pass on what they learned to others. This creates a chain reaction of positive behaviour that can lift entire communities. It shows that real leadership is not about giving orders or demanding attention; it's about living in a way that inspires others to be better versions of themselves.

Even small acts can create an enormous impact. Leadership shines brightest in the little moments that often go unnoticed. A leader who picks up trash after an event, treats every volunteer with dignity, listens patiently to the concerns of a young person, or stands up quietly but firmly against injustice sends a louder and clearer message than grand speeches ever could. Such moments teach that true leadership is rooted in service, not in status. It teaches that being great is not about being above others, but about lifting others up.

Positive role models also raise the aspirations of young people. When youth see someone who looks like them, who shares their background and values, succeeding while staying true to their faith and character, it expands their belief in what is possible. It removes the limits they may have unknowingly placed on themselves. Instead of thinking, "Success is not for people like me," they start to believe, "If they can do it, so can I." This shift in mindset is crucial. It turns hesitation into ambition, fear into hope, and uncertainty into action.

Moreover, good role models don't just demonstrate success; they demonstrate resilience. Life is full of challenges, setbacks, and failures. When youth see their role models facing difficulties with patience, perseverance, and trust in Allah (SWT), it teaches them how to handle their own struggles. It shows that failure is not the end, but a stepping stone. It encourages youth to keep striving, even when things get tough, knowing that success is often born through persistence and faith.

In the Muslim community, the responsibility of being a positive role model is especially significant. Every action, whether big or small, becomes an opportunity to teach and inspire. Parents, teachers, community leaders, and even older siblings have countless chances each day to lead by example. Their consistency, their sincerity, and their commitment to Islamic principles serve as living lessons that shape the next generation.

Finally, it's important to recognise that no one is perfect. Youth do not need perfect role models; they need authentic ones. Role models who admit their mistakes, seek forgiveness, and continuously strive to improve teach one of the most important lessons—that growth is a lifelong journey. By being honest and humble, positive role models show that true greatness lies not in never falling, but in rising after every fall with greater strength and faith.

In conclusion, positive role modelling is one of the most powerful tools for influencing youth behaviour and aspirations. It lights a path that young people can follow with confidence. It nurtures values, strengthens character, and inspires dreams rooted in faith and integrity. Positive role models help build stronger individuals, healthier communities, and a brighter future for all by embodying the virtues they wish to see in the next generation.

Fostering Mentorship Networks and Peer Support Among Young Leaders

Mentorship is often seen as something that flows from older to younger generations, with wisdom being passed down over time. While this traditional model is invaluable, it's important to recognise that mentorship doesn't always have to come from elders. Some of the most impactful mentorship can actually happen between peers—young people supporting, challenging, and inspiring one another. Peer mentorship creates a dynamic sense of unity, belonging, and shared growth that strengthens individuals and communities alike.

When young leaders come together in peer support networks, something powerful happens. They exchange fresh ideas, challenge one another to aim higher, and constantly remind each other of their greater purpose. These interactions are not only about learning skills; they are about building resilience, fostering teamwork, and developing mutual respect. Peer mentorship allows leadership to feel less lonely and more communal. It transforms leadership from an isolated burden into a shared journey, where each young person lifts others as they climb.

Building these networks requires intentional effort. Communities can play a crucial role by creating spaces and programs encouraging peer-to-peer mentorship. Leadership circles, youth-led projects, and mentorship initiatives where slightly older youth guide and support younger ones can make a major difference. Mosques, Islamic centres, student associations, and community groups all have the potential to become hubs for these life-changing connections. By providing the structure and encouragement for youth to mentor one another, communities invest in the collective strength of their future leaders.

Organised efforts like youth conferences, workshops, community service projects, and leadership camps can bring young Muslims together in meaningful ways. These experiences allow them to collaborate, brainstorm, and solve real-world problems side by side. Over time, they build relationships rooted in trust and mutual inspiration. Peer mentorship naturally develops when young people have repeated opportunities to see each other's strengths, witness each other's growth, and offer each other sincere advice and support.

In today's world, technology also plays an essential role in connecting youth beyond physical spaces. Online platforms open doors to global peer mentorship networks. Through group chats, virtual meetings, and social media communities, young Muslims from different countries can share their journeys, discuss their successes and struggles, and exchange strategies for leadership and personal growth. A young leader in Malaysia can inspire one in Canada. A student activist in South Africa can support a budding youth organiser in the United Kingdom. Distance is no longer a barrier when the goal is unity and collective development.

Virtual mentorship circles can be especially helpful for youth who feel isolated in their local communities. When a young Muslim doesn't find like-minded peers nearby, online spaces can provide critical encouragement and motivation. Digital platforms enable the exchange of resources, experiences, and spiritual reminders that nurture both leadership skills and faith. They also teach youth how to adapt, communicate effectively, and think globally while acting locally.

One of the greatest lessons peer mentorship teaches is the art of uplifting others. In nurturing one another, young leaders learn the true meaning of leadership: service, humility, and compassion. They become each other's sources of strength and resilience. They understand that leadership is not about personal achievement alone but about bringing others along the journey, about making space for different voices, and about ensuring that no one is left behind. This collective leadership model is one of the most powerful forces for positive change. When youth are taught to lead with others, not just for others, they build movements, not just moments.

Every young Muslim has the potential to be a leader—not necessarily by holding an official title, but by making a meaningful impact wherever they are. Leadership begins in small actions: offering a helping hand, standing up for what is right, encouraging a struggling friend, or organising a local charity drive. By nurturing mentorship and positive role modelling within peer groups, we prepare young Muslims not just to take charge but to lead with purpose, sincerity, and faith. We remind them that leadership in Islam is an amanah—a trust and a responsibility to serve others and uphold justice.

The future of the Muslim community depends on what we nurture today. If we surround our youth with positive mentors, empower them with supportive networks, and constantly remind them of their incredible potential, we are equipping them with the tools they need to thrive—not only in this world but also in the Hereafter. Our investment in mentorship today will shape generations of compassionate, courageous, and capable leaders who serve both their communities and their Creator with excellence.

Let's commit to building these networks intentionally. Let us empower young people not just with leadership skills but with living examples of integrity, faith, and service. Let us create spaces where they can learn from one another, lift one another, and inspire one another. Let them grow under the light of those who have walked the path before them and shine bright for the generations yet to come.

Peer mentorship is not just an option; it's an essential ingredient for building strong, vibrant Muslim communities. By encouraging youth to lead together, we ensure that our future is filled with leaders who are grounded in their faith, committed to justice, and driven by a sincere desire to make the world a better place—for everyone.

Chapter Eleven

Empowering Muslim Youth for a Promising Future

Empowerment Strategies for Nurturing Future Muslim Leaders

Empowering young Muslims begins with a clear understanding of who they are and what they are capable of. Within every youth lies the strength to lead, to uplift others, and to contribute meaningfully to their community. But that potential must be nurtured with care, wisdom, and faith.

The journey to empowerment starts by believing in youth—not just as tomorrow's leaders but as today's change makers. To nurture them effectively, we must provide an environment where they feel seen, heard, and supported. Mentorship programs, access to knowledge, safe spaces for discussion, and faith-based leadership development are essential tools in this process.

At the heart of all empowerment is trust. When adults trust youth with responsibility and guidance, they rise to the occasion. Letting young people take the lead in community service projects, youth events, or peer mentoring not only builds their confidence but also teaches real-life leadership.

Moreover, empowerment means teaching youth how to think critically, speak confidently, and live with integrity. It means grounding them in Islamic teachings while encouraging creativity, innovation, and self-expression. When we empower youth with knowledge and purpose, we equip them to lead in both the spiritual and worldly spheres.

Investing in Youth Education, Training, and Leadership Programs

Education is the foundation of empowerment. But this education must go beyond school textbooks. It must include life skills, character building, and spiritual growth. When we invest in youth through diverse educational opportunities, we are not only securing their futures—we are uplifting the future of the entire ummah.

Leadership training programs for Muslim youth are among the most effective ways to prepare them for real-world challenges. These programs can include workshops on communication, conflict resolution, time management, and decision-making—all delivered through the lens of Islamic values.

Equally important are Islamic knowledge programs that help youth connect with their deen. Understanding the Quran, learning from the Seerah of the Prophet (PBUH), and exploring Islamic history gives young Muslims a deep sense of identity and direction. It roots them in something greater than themselves, which is critical in a world full of distractions.

Youth camps, community seminars, and student leadership forums are also effective platforms. These experiences connect young Muslims with mentors and peers who share their faith and passion for growth. They learn to collaborate, serve others, and think as leaders.

We must also invest in creating online platforms and digital content that meet youth where they are. In the digital age, engaging them through podcasts, videos, apps, and virtual programs can keep them connected to knowledge, faith, and community wherever they go.

Providing Opportunities for Youth to Showcase Talents and Initiatives

Muslim youth are talented, innovative, and full of ideas—but they need opportunities to shine. One of the most powerful ways to empower them is by giving them platforms to share their skills and passions with the world. Whether it's through public speaking competitions, art and writing contests, community service awards, or youth entrepreneurship fairs, showcasing youth-led initiatives builds confidence and creates a ripple effect of inspiration.

When young Muslims see that their contributions are valued, they feel motivated to do more. They become role models for their peers and start seeing themselves as active participants in society, not just observers. Local mosques and Islamic centres should actively create events led by youth. From organising fundraisers for humanitarian causes to leading halaqas or Friday youth nights, these experiences are vital. They teach responsibility, foster initiative, and provide a healthy outlet for energy and creativity.

Even small responsibilities—like setting up prayer spaces, organising charity drives, or creating youth newsletters—can instill a sense of purpose. These opportunities not only showcase talent but also allow young people to connect their actions to their faith. When we celebrate youth accomplishments and provide ongoing support, we encourage a culture of growth, resilience, and excellence rooted in Islamic values.

Vision for the Future: Inspiring Youth to Lead with Purpose and Passion

Empowerment without vision is like a ship without a compass. To truly inspire young Muslims, we must help them envision a future that is meaningful, impactful, and rooted in purpose. This begins by encouraging them to dream big—while staying grounded in Islamic teachings. The vision we offer youth should not be limited to personal success, but expanded to include service, justice, and the betterment of society.

We must ask our youth powerful questions: What change do you want to see in the world? How can you serve your community better? How can your talents uplift others? When young people are challenged to think this way, they begin to understand that their lives matter not just for their own benefit, but for the sake of the ummah and humanity.

Purpose-driven youth lead with sincerity and strength. They don't just follow trends—they set them. They don't wait for others to act—they take initiative. And their leadership becomes a beacon for others, especially in times of hardship or confusion.

By inspiring our youth to lead with passion and purpose, we ignite the fire to serve Allah (SWT) and His creation with excellence. Their goals become clearer, their actions more focused, and their journey more rewarding.

Encouraging Youth to Envision Positive Change and Contribute to the Ummah

Every generation carries the responsibility of uplifting the ummah, and this generation of youth is no different. But before they can contribute, they must be taught to believe in their ability to make a difference. Positive change doesn't always start with big movements. Often, it begins with small, consistent actions. A young person standing up against bullying or helping classmates understand prayer times—all these acts build a stronger, more compassionate community.

Youth must be encouraged to identify the issues that matter most to them—whether it's climate justice, educational equity, poverty, mental health, or Islamophobia—and take small but impactful steps toward improvement. These steps include awareness campaigns, school projects, volunteer work, or starting a youth podcast discussing relevant social and spiritual issues.

This active engagement fosters responsibility and nurtures a lifelong habit of service. It shows youth that they are not powerless. On the contrary, their voice matters. Their presence in the community is vital. Their perspective is unique and needed.

Muslim youth are in a position to bridge gaps—between cultures, between generations, and between tradition and modernity. By encouraging them to think globally but act locally, we help them build bridges of understanding, service, and solidarity. And as they take action, their contributions become part of the legacy of the ummah—a legacy of compassion, justice, and truth.

Empowering Young Muslims to Be Ambassadors of Faith and Goodwill in Society

The modern world is full of stereotypes and misunderstandings about Islam. One of the most powerful responses to this is not debate—but example. When Muslim youth lead lives of kindness, excellence, and integrity, they become walking ambassadors of their faith.

Empowering youth to represent Islam with dignity means teaching them how to articulate their beliefs confidently, respond to challenges with wisdom, and stand tall in their identity. It means reminding them that wherever they go, they carry not just their name but their values.

When a Muslim student excels in academics and helps peers, when a young Muslim professional treats colleagues with fairness and respect, or when a young activist campaigns for justice with sincerity—they send a message louder than any speech. They show that Islam is not just a religion of rituals, but a way of life rooted in peace, justice, and service.

Encouraging Muslim youth to see themselves as representatives of their deen is not about placing pressure—it's about unlocking honour. It's about showing them that being Muslim is a source of pride, not shame. That their faith can empower them to be better humans, better leaders, and better contributors to society.

By supporting youth in embracing their identity, engaging with their communities, and living with purpose, we prepare them to face the world not with fear—but with faith. Empowering Muslim youth isn't just a duty—it's an investment in our collective future. It's about planting seeds of hope, strength, and leadership that will grow into trees of justice, knowledge, and compassion.

With the right guidance, opportunities, and vision, our youth can become the builders of a brighter ummah and a better world. It starts with believing in them, supporting them, and walking beside them as they discover who they are and what they can become. Let us raise a generation that is proud of its faith, confident in its purpose, and ready to lead—not just for the sake of leadership, but for the sake of Allah (SWT) and the betterment of all humanity. The future is in their hands. Let's empower them to shape it with wisdom, courage, and faith.

Chapter Twelve

Conclusion

As we reach the end of this journey, take a moment to reflect on more than just the lessons learned. True leadership is not about titles or achievements; it's a reflection of your character, your faith, and your commitment to serving a purpose greater than yourself. For Muslim youth, leadership is a sacred trust—a responsibility to uphold truth, act with kindness, and inspire others through sincerity and strength of heart.

Throughout these pages, you've walked through the lives of courageous young Muslims who changed the course of history. You have explored the principles of leadership rooted in the Quran and Sunnah and uncovered the traits that elevate ordinary individuals into remarkable guides. These lessons are not meant to remain words on a page; they are seeds planted within you. They're meant to shape the way you speak, act, and navigate the world. You're capable of being a force for good, a light in times of uncertainty, and a source of strength when it's needed most.

Leadership begins within. It starts with mastering your own impulses, choosing patience over anger, conviction over compromise, and mercy over pride. It's not about seeking recognition but striving to please Allah (SWT) with pure intentions and steadfastness. Your efforts may not always be seen or rewarded right away. There will be moments of loneliness, doubt, and trials. Yet, remember, the companions of the

Prophet (PBUH) did not reach greatness through ease but through perseverance, sacrifice, and unwavering faith.

You are part of that same noble legacy. Whether your dreams lead you to build organisations, teach, create, innovate, or serve, you carry the power to impact lives through your values. Leadership is not confined to stages and titles. It's found in classrooms, mosques, neighbourhoods, homes, and even in the online spaces you inhabit. Every encounter is a chance to reflect the beauty of Islam through your character.

Don't wait for perfection or permission to begin. True leadership comes from a heart willing to act, grow, and stand firm even when the path is unclear. Leadership is a continuous journey, not a final destination. Some days, you'll lead with bold action; other days, with quiet resilience. Both are valuable. Both are needed.

Surround yourself with those who encourage your growth. Find mentors who live with integrity. Be the kind of friend who lifts others and listens with an open heart. Build habits of service, humility, and forgiveness. These habits not only make great leaders but also make great people.

The ummah needs you. The world needs you. Not flawless, but passionate and purposeful. You are the bridge between the struggles of the past and the hopes of the future. Let your leadership be measured by the lives you touch and the principles you uphold. Walk forward with courage, faith, and the deep knowledge that Allah (SWT) guides every sincere step. You are ready. Be the Leader of Faith you were created to be—and let the world feel your light.

Find Out More

Website: www.barakahinbusiness.com

Socials: @barakahinbusiness

If you enjoyed this book, kindly leave a review to help expand our reach so others may benefit also.

www.ingramcontent.com/pod-product-compliance
Lightning Source LLC
Chambersburg PA
CBHW052211090526
44584CB00019BA/3030